THE LONG WAY AROUND

THE LONG WAY AROUND

stories and sermons from a life's journey

To Marcia Ginsberg

I hope you enjoy and find this meaningful.

Robert Dobrusin

ISBN: 1540304256
ISBN 13: 9781540304254
Library of Congress Control Number: 2016918920
CreateSpace Independent Publishing Platform
North Charleston, South Carolina

For Ellie: May we always travel down the road together

"Now when Pharaoh let the people go, God did not lead them by way of the land of the Philistines although it was nearer"... (Exodus 13:17)

Introduction

I was ordained as a rabbi a few days before my 27th birthday. It's hard to believe that this happened over 30 years ago. It has been a wonderful journey with, I pray, more roads to come.

They say time flies when you're having fun and, while each day hasn't exactly been "fun," I am grateful each and every day for the opportunities the rabbinate brings me.

When I stand under the *huppah*, I often say to the couple: "For a rabbi, it just doesn't get any better than this." This comes from the heart. Knowing that I play an important part in the holiest day of a person's life is as satisfying a role as I can imagine. And I could say the same for other moments of family or personal joy or sadness that I have participated in.

But sometimes, weeks can go by without such an experience, and it is then that I count on the other most satisfying experience I have as a rabbi: the opportunity to deliver a sermon. For this rabbi, this is a thrill that has never grown old.

Despite the welcomed trend to make organized religion a conversation rather than an authoritative monologue, and despite contemporary society's insistence that we say everything we need to say in less than 140 characters, I still believe that the sermon is a most effective way to share, inspire, and educate. I truly love to write and deliver sermons, and I have been blessed with congregants who are eager to learn, happy to be challenged, and, most importantly, willing to put up with my tendency to take them the "long way around" to get to my point. After all, as in life, where a long roundabout journey is often rewarded with a significant experience or achievement, a major part of the drama in a good sermon is the path traveled to get to the main idea.

When I write my sermons, I try to take people on the journey with me, and often the long journey to the main idea involves a reference to a particular contemporary reality that might, at first, seem to have absolutely nothing to do with anything worth teaching from the *bima*. It is then that I count on the congregation's patience to trust that we will eventually reach the intended destination.

But in addition to those contemporary references, sometimes there is something else behind the sermon, something that I may not want to share publicly. Indeed, many of my sermons derive from personal experiences which have directed and shaped my thoughts in a particular way.

Some of my sermons have roots in "ancient" history – from the earliest days of my childhood. Others develop from more recent memories. Whichever it is, the truth is that I start many sermons in the middle of a story, leaving unsaid what has led me to talk about the subject at hand.

So, often a personal story is behind what I speak about and I usually don't let the listener in on the back-story– until now, that is.

This is where this book comes in.

This book is about who I am and where I have come from. It is about how the stories I remember, the interests I have, and the unique idiosyncrasies of my life have led to the sermons I most deeply treasure.

I hope the reader will find the stories enjoyable and engaging. They are dear to me but I'm quite sure that there is nothing so unique about my life's stories that alone would make for an interesting book. The focus of this book is on how the stories and the sermons intersect. I believe this demonstrates the ways our personal experiences can lead to lessons that we can share with those around us.

The sermons speak for themselves. But let me share a few words about the stories. They are all true as I remember them, and they are told with love and reverence for the family members involved. I write with the deepest respect for the memory of my parents and grandmother, and dearly hope that this is clear in these pages. Telling these stories is an expression of gratitude. I thank my parents for their encouragement to pursue my writing while they were on this earth and I honestly believe they still encourage me to tell my stories.

I also write about the people who so closely surround me in life today. Their love and support are behind every page and every story.

I could have gone on page after page about my relationship with my big brother, Charley, but I'll leave many of those stories for him to tell in his own book. Suffice it to say that I have looked up to Charley since the day I was born. I treasure the bond between us and thank him profusely for the many times he has influenced my thinking and challenged me with his wisdom.

I could not begin to imagine what my world would be like without my children. Avi and Mickie: I love you both with all of my heart and am so thankful for what you have brought me. Thank you for allowing me to share *some* of our stories.

And as for my dear wife Ellen, while I don't generally believe that God micromanages our lives, I make an exception in this one case. I thank God each day for bringing me to Ann Arbor and leading me to an apartment around the corner from the house Ellen had bought a year before. I can't begin to thank you enough, Ellie, for inspiring me and encouraging me to write this book. I look forward to so many more chapters in our life together.

I also want to express my appreciation to my congregants, first in Lansdale, Pennsylvania and for the last 28 years in Ann Arbor, Michigan, whose interest in my sermons has inspired me to take such writing seriously. Thank you also to my friends everywhere who have encouraged me in this undertaking and critiqued my work.

Thank you also to Sarah Wood for her invaluable editorial assistance and suggestions in helping to bring to fruition my dream of telling these stories.

Rabbis are fortunate in that we have a stage from which to tell our stories. But the truth is that each and every one of us has stories which we can share to teach the lessons we have learned. I hope this book inspires readers to find the stage from which to tell their own stories and teach the lessons they have learned to all who will listen.

And with that, the stories begin…

1

Lessons from the Rubble

I begin my story at the beginning: with my father, Manny Dobrusin. I sometimes think I got the "rabbi gene" from my father. Dad should have been a rabbi. He loved to be on a pulpit of any kind. He loved Judaism and loved to preach about its lessons, most notably *responsibility*, which he called: "The Jewish Mantra."

He also loved to lecture people who weren't quite living up to his standards of responsibility, something most rabbis can't get away with easily today.

Most importantly, though, like all rabbis, he loved to teach.

Dad was a fantastic teacher. Of course, as is true of any teacher, he was not always successful in his efforts. On countless occasions, he would try to teach *me* something and within five minutes would throw up his hands and call me "Stoop," a term of endearment, I always assumed. Or, he would wave his hands theatrically saying: "I give up, the boy will never learn!"

You name it and he tried to teach it to me. Of course, there was driving, but that was only one subject in the curriculum. An abridged list of my failed courses might include: using a screwdriver (or any other tool for that matter), bleeding the air out of the water heater in the cellar, writing a proper letter in the days when such things were important, putting in storm windows...the list goes on and on. He taught. I failed to learn. Almost every time.

But there were two things my father did manage to teach me successfully. One was the art of playing the card game cribbage, a feat I have not been able to replicate with my wife or kids but which, thanks to a "cribbage app," comes in handy when writer's block sets in. Playing a game or ten helps the ideas flow a bit more easily.

And, secondly, Dad taught me how to travel.

Manny Dobrusin was a "Renaissance Man" in many ways and one of his greatest talents, largely unappreciated to anyone outside of family and close friends, was planning and executing memorable family vacations. He firmly believed that travel done correctly – his way – was an essential experience of life. As a result, we always had family trips to look forward to.

The trips we took when we were kids were unforgettable, mostly because of my father's mastering two of the most important rules of travel and perhaps of life as well. First, he believed in planning carefully; and, secondly, he steadfastly maintained the absolute conviction that the trip would be worthwhile, no matter how it started out or where it seemed headed.

What was Dad's formula for taking a trip? Combine planning and determination with a solid knowledge of history and grasp of mechanical science basics; add to this an insistence on doing things that made sense to him even if they didn't to anyone else; throw in some spontaneous, biting humor, occasionally self-deprecating, but more often aimed at everyone else, and, voila!, you have Manny Dobrusin, Family Traveler Extraordinaire!

Dad would get an idea for a trip and almost immediately a box would appear on the dining room table. For the next few months, the box would be filled with travel folders, hotel brochures, maps, and anything else that he could get for free. He would spend weeks and weeks planning for the trip – choosing all of the motels in advance, knowing exactly where we would be and when. Then, the big day would arrive and, after filming an opening scene of the vacation movie featuring my brother and I standing next to the car holding up a carefully hand-written sign indicating the itinerary, off we went.

Actually, our first family vacations weren't road trips. Dad must have felt that we weren't quite ready for the open road, so we spent several summers when I was very young in a small cottage at the beach in Winthrop, an old oceanfront town next to Boston.

While it wouldn't satisfy my later desire to wander, I learned to love vacations while spending the summer on Neptune Avenue. I have vague memories of life in the tiny house we stayed in, set back at the end of a walkway a half block down from the beach. I remember walking hand in hand with my mother along the oceanfront road. I remember Molly's, the small variety store at the end of our street with its green door which slammed shut behind you and bounced back a bit before slamming a second time.

I also remember weekly trips to the next town, Revere, and its honky-tonk amusement boardwalk. I loved that place, even though one night the whole top to my first slice of pizza slid off right onto my leg. It burned me pretty badly but it didn't sour me on Revere Beach or summer vacations.

My brother has often told me about one unforgettable moment that I must have been too young to appreciate. One time my father loaded everything we needed for the summer into the car but didn't leave room for himself. It was an educational moment as Charley heard words he had never heard before. My mother was sitting behind the wheel as Dad stormed away, took the bus and met us there. In addition to displaying frustration and embarrassment, Dad showed quite a bit of courage, as leaving my mother to find her way anywhere beyond a mile or two from home was tempting fate. Despite the risk, the family reunited at the beach safe and sound.

Winthrop was fun. But we were growing up and the little cottage seemed much too small. It was time to take our show on the road.

I was seven years old when we went on our first family road trip: to the White Mountains of New Hampshire. We spent three nights in three different motels within a 25-mile radius of each other. That might seem a bit ridiculous but that made it more of a trip, Dad thought. Our days were spent seeing small stores or museums, walking through various tourist traps while looking at the beautiful views and, in my father's words: "sitting on the side of a mountain and belching," his expression for doing whatever he pleased.

I can trace my life-long love for travel directly to one particular moment on the first morning of that trip. Sitting by myself at about 6 a.m. on the front step of cabin 14 in a "motor court" in North Woodstock, New Hampshire, I pretended that I was the host of the "Today" show broadcasting from that choice location. To me it was paradise. It didn't matter that the place looked nothing like what was pictured in the brochure, or that the promised "luxurious" swimming pool was unusable because it hadn't been inflated properly. I had been bitten by the travel bug and I never looked back.

The three day trip was unforgettable. We took the tramway to the top of Cannon Mountain and then sat at the base of several other mountains watching the cable cars and gondolas go up and down. I'm not quite sure why we were supposed to find that enjoyable. I suppose my parents believed that once you had done something, you could then vicariously enjoy the experience that others were having going up and down the mountainside without doing it a second time.

Besides, it was cheaper.

We visited a place called Clark's Trading Post that featured trained bears standing on a small pedestal high off the ground. I'm not quite sure how they got them to go up there. But once there, those bears operated a pulley that brought cans of bear food up to the pedestal. Quite a thrill for this city boy!

I remember visiting a place called the Morse Museum. I'm not quite sure why my father wanted to take us there but when I think about it, I have vague memories of masks and spears. I searched for the museum on the Internet several years ago only to find it had closed down. But as I correctly recalled, it had been a repository of artifacts from the owner's trips around the world, especially on safari in Africa. The Morse Museum probably was as close to Africa, or any place outside of North America for that matter, that my father ever saw. We were bored but he loved it.

We visited the Flume Gorge and Lost River, two beautiful places with somewhat demanding hikes. This assumes, however, that one walked the entire trail, which of course we never did. But most memorable was our pilgrimage to the "Holy of Holies," the Old Man of the Mountain, the natural rock formation high on a mountaintop in Franconia Notch State Park which served as the symbol of the State of New Hampshire.

The Old Man made quite an impression on me. Truthfully, he gave me "the creeps," but I couldn't take my eyes off him.

Forty-four years later and a few years after my father had died, I took our then 12-year-old daughter Mickie on a trip to New Hampshire. After years in Michigan, it was time to go back again and I was pleasantly surprised by what I found.

The mountain views are still there. The Flume is still there and we did the whole hike, thank you. We actually drove through the town that housed the Morse Museum but Mickie made it clear that she didn't want to waste time looking for its former location: a wise child indeed. Clark's Trading Post is still there and there are still bears on the pedestals but now its gift shop has expanded and they have "bumper boats." The tramway still goes up Cannon Mountain, but I suppose part of its charm is that it is an "old fashioned" experience. We passed by the previously referred to "motor court" which was still in business with a vastly improved swimming pool.

It was wonderful to go back in time and to see everything.

But the most important place, the object of our original pilgrimage, the Old Man of the Mountain, wasn't there. He had disappeared, collapsing into the valley below in May of 2003.

It was a shock to me at the time and it inspired a sermon I delivered before Yizkor, the memorial service on Yom Kippur, four months later. The sermon pays homage to the Old Man of the Mountain and to another old man as well.

A TRIBUTE TO TWO OLD MEN
YOM KIPPUR 2003

I lost something dear to me this past year.

When I heard the news, I called my brother immediately because I knew that he would feel as I did.

I was not surprised. He took it very hard.

And so we talked. And as we talked, we remembered.

We talked about the pilgrimage we took each year when we were kids. Sometimes, we went at the beginning or end of a trip to someplace else. Sometimes, we took the eight-hour round trip in one day.

It was the same each time.

My father would park the car and we would get out and stand by a beautiful blue lake and look up into the mountains.

*And there it was. Or, more properly, there **he** was: the Great Stone Face, the Profile, the Old Man of the Mountain presiding over Franconia Notch State Park in the White Mountains of New Hampshire.*

There, high on a mountaintop, was an outcropping of rocks, a few strangely shaped stones that nature had carved into the unmistakable face of an old man, jaw jutted out, resolutely looking off into the distance.

In 1939, Robert F. Doane wrote these words:

**"On the crest of a mighty mountain, looking over the lake below
A face with a human expression watches many a century go.
It was made from a mountain of granite
With the skill of a sculptor's hand
And guards the green valley below it
As time passes over the land."**

Then there are the unforgettable words of Daniel Webster:

"Men hang out their signs indicative of their respective trades; shoe makers hang out a gigantic shoe; jewelers a monster watch, and the dentist hangs out a gold tooth; but up in the

Mountains of New Hampshire, God Almighty has hung out a sign to show that there He makes men."

The Old Man was always there.

Then, this past May, on a foggy, chilly morning, the stones broke off from the cliff, rumbled into the valley below. The Old Man was gone.

Reflecting on the life of a human being, the Psalmist wrote in Psalm 103: "The wind passes over it and it is gone and no one can recognize where it grew."

And now time passes over the mountains and all we can do is recognize where the Old Man stood. It is not the same. We will never see him again. All we have is the memory.

The story of the Old Man has moved me so deeply because it reminds me of my youth, my beloved New England, the mountains that I love so much and miss so dearly and, of course, my father, may he rest in peace.

But it moves me for another reason as well. It moves me because the Old Man of the Mountain has a story to tell.

We know our lives are finite. We need Yom Kippur to come around every year to remind us of it, but in our hearts, we always know it.

We also know that human-made objects crumble.

But we don't expect to see the natural world change before our eyes.

And yet God has told us that the natural world would also crumble before us at times.

The prophet Isaiah teaches: "For the mountains may move and the hills be shaken but my love for you will not disappear says the Lord."

This verse reminds us that everything on earth will change one day: the change of seasons, an earthquake, a windstorm, erosion, evolution, growth, aging and, ultimately, death. Everything is on its way to change.

Sometimes we see change coming and try to stop it. In fact, the Old Man of the Mountain was held together for years with cables to keep him from falling. But, in the end, the force of time was stronger than the *cables trying to hold time back and the Old Man tumbled to the ground below.*

I still long for his presence. I still want to go back to that spot. I still want to go back to New Hampshire and I want to lift up my eyes to the mountains and remember what was there.

For that is the blessing of memory.

All of us one day will stand with a figurative pile of rubble around us, looking desperately for the face which comforted, for the eyes that brought joy, for the smile that welcomed us, for the hands that held us, for the feet that walked alongside, wishing beyond all hope that they were there. But we won't find them there and we think we won't find life anywhere because nothing could be found in the fallen rubble around us.

At that moment of sadness, we might find comfort in the words of the Psalmist: "I will lift up my eyes to the mountains, from where will my help come?"

Many read this verse as a theological statement, referring to one who took comfort in the stability of nature, symbolized by the mountains, and saw God's presence in that stability.

But the problem with that interpretation, as beautiful as it is, is that it based on a fallacy. Nothing, not even a mountain, lasts forever. Nothing is permanent if we wait long enough. Everything is changing.

Perhaps, then, the point of the verse is exactly the opposite of what we might first think.

The verse tells us to look to the mountains and see that even as they surely change, God does not change. God keeps watch. God's love and loyalty still stands firm. In fact, it is the only reality that is unchanging.

That is a message for all of us as we consider the people that we love. Cherish those you have, allow them to change as you yourself change, but let the bonds between you be as strong as the cables that can hold back rocks.

Then, when the time comes – and it will one day – when even the strongest of holds isn't strong enough and death takes the person we love away, let us never be afraid, in time, to go back to the spot we knew, near a life-giving pool of water, look up to the mountains and remember.

Let us also remember that the Psalmist was so deeply and so profoundly wrong when he said: "the wind passes over it and it is gone and no one can recognize where it grew." Everyone recognizes where a human life grew, and the memory of that life is a reminder that here on earth, God almighty makes human beings and their mark is made to continue long after they die.

And let us remember that though the face may be gone, the memory still shines through the rubble that we think our lives have become and that memory urges us in time to stand up, shake off the dust of mourning and resolutely look forward again.

May the memory of the Old Man of the Mountain and, more importantly, the memory of all the men and women we hold in our hearts be for a blessing. May we never forget the lessons they have taught us. And may we continue to look to the mountains and to the heavens beyond and feel their presence – and God's presence – always.

As I traveled in New Hampshire with Mickie, I realized once again that her life is very different from mine. I grew up with a thick Boston accent, her accent is subtly Midwestern. I am a passionate Red Sox fan and she professes to love the Tigers, and she knows it frustrates me like crazy. I grew up trudging up the hills of Boston and, as a kid, her idea of a "hill" was the little bump on the street next to ours.

But on that trip, she seemed to love New England and that is not insignificant.

By the time she was 12, Mickie had been in more states and put in more air miles than I had at three times her age. She has had experiences I have never had, including two family white water rafting trips which were so scary my parents wouldn't have even let us stand on the river bank to watch them.

So, I was worried that, after having been to Grand Teton, Yellowstone, and Alaska, the White Mountains wouldn't seem that big a deal for her or for me. Yet there we were, riding the state highways and back roads of New Hampshire with her looking up and enjoying the same mountains I did when I was a kid and, as much as I loved Grand Teton, this is more real and this is home. Apparently even my Michigan-born daughter could feel it because, as we were driving, she asked me to tell her stories about her Papa Dobrusin whom she remembers only vaguely.

As I told her the stories, she laughed hysterically, even at the parts that weren't supposed to be funny. I told her about how hard it was for Dad to be a salesman because he was so honest. I told her about the songs he wrote which brought him peace until his dying day. I shared with her some of my father's best extemporaneous lines and the stories that go with them.

Then, in a remarkable gesture for a 12-year-old girl (and those who have been there know what I mean), she reached out and touched my hand and said: "You miss him, don't you?"

Yes, Mickie, I do miss him.

Then, we arrived at the lookout point to see where the Old Man of the Mountain used to be. We looked at the pictures on the sign and looked up to the mountains. He wasn't there. He is gone.

But you can see where he was and, if you look carefully enough, you know he still lives on.

That family trip to New Hampshire took place in 1963, the year after John Glenn orbited the earth. For Dad, the New Hampshire trip was like the flights of Project Mercury: the beginning of the manned space program. It was a time to work out the kinks and perfect the art of family travel.

Like the space program, our journeys became more ambitious each subsequent year: a week in Canada, New York for the 1964 World's Fair, and finally, when I was 11, the ultimate expedition: a two-week trip to Pennsylvania Dutch Country, Williamsburg, Washington DC, and Philadelphia with countless stops in between.

The first moon landing was still three years away when my father's ambitious plan came to fruition. With apologies to Neil Armstrong, the Washington trip was a giant leap for the Dobrusin family and Dad took great pride in the successful effort.

My parents, my grandmother, my brother, and I were joined on this trip by my Grandmother's cousin or life-long friend – we were never sure which – Aunt Frances, who came along to keep Nana company and to make the motel arrangements a little more manageable.

Faced with the prospect of traveling with 6, Dad rented a Dodge Polara station wagon with a fancy roof luggage rack. The car's best feature was a marvelous new invention: a rear seat that faced backwards. The plan was that my brother and I would have our own territory in that rear seat. It would be our "headquarters" for the next 14 days and, the night before we left, we set it up just the way we wanted: with plenty of MAD magazines, piles of snacks, and paper and pens to write private notes making fun of the other passengers.

Then the big day arrived. At the crack of dawn, we piled into the car and off we went. Well, not quite yet…

Two rituals had to be performed before we could really begin our trip. The first you already know: the obligatory family movie with a sign, in my mother's fanciest printing, indicating each planned stop. The entire neighborhood gathered to see the sight as we waved good-bye to Massachusetts. Then we were off. Well, not really. While the open road beckoned, it would have to wait. We were obligated to observe the second Dobrusin Family "beginning of the trip" tradition: eating breakfast at Howard Johnson's once we got on the Mass Turnpike.

It didn't matter that we had eaten a "light" breakfast before leaving the house. We had to stop. To be fair, since the filming of the departure scene took an hour and a half or so, it had probably been three hours since we ate when we pulled into HoJo's about 15 miles from home.

Then, with our hunger satisfied at last, my brother and I settled into the "way back" seat. Charley fell asleep and I kept myself entertained by singing *Yellow Submarine* 10 or 15 times over while holding a clipboard on which I meticulously kept a list of every town we passed through.

Looking out the back window, waving at the cars, two rows away from our parents and from my father's silly songs, and one row behind my grandmother's constant chattering and complaining … it was just paradise. I had never been so happy.

Our first overnight stop was just outside of New York City. We could have driven further but the plan was not to overdo it on the first day, so we checked into a motel for the night. It was here, in this place that I had one of the foundational experiences of my youth. I will forever remember this motel as the site of a moment similar to the expulsion from the Garden of Eden. Paradise ended for me at the Holiday Inn in Spring Valley, New York.

While unpacking the roof rack, Dad realized, with a burst of borderline profanity, that it would take an enormous effort to take the luggage down from the rack and put it back up every day. He tossed and turned that night cursing himself for not thinking of this during the intricate planning stages of the mission. Suddenly the inspiration came for a "mid-course correction" as the astronauts so deftly call it when they have to make an adjustment.

The next morning, we found that Dad had folded down the "way back" seats taking away our territory. He put all of the luggage in the newly created trunk and we all sat in the two front rows of seats. Paradise was lost and it was one of my first introductions to one tenet of the Dobrusin family philosophy: when the kids think things are perfect, something needs to be changed.

Driving a non-air conditioned station wagon filled with six people in the heat of summer (and I should, as tactfully as I can, mention that we were not particularly svelte people) with luggage piled where two extra seats should be while a fancy luggage rack sat empty on top didn't bother my father in principle. He certainly never cared how silly something looked to other people as long as it made sense to him. Someday I'll be able to fully relate the story about the elaborate, architecturally conceived basketball hoop he designed for our back yard which was such an eyesore that it became a neighborhood tourist attraction. But it's still too painful for me to talk about.

No. Dad never cared how something looked. But that night he was still restless; something else was bothering him.

He woke up wondering aloud: "What would happen if we got a flat tire?" He'd have to take all of the luggage out of the trunk in order to get at the spare tire which was now completely covered with suitcases. So, the next morning, in a moment of genius, Dad took the spare tire out, put *it* on the fancy luggage rack and put the luggage back into the trunk. Now we had a car packed with luggage and six good-sized people squeezed into two rows of seats with a spare tire sitting on the top of the car.

Somehow, we couldn't get across to him how utterly ridiculous this looked. Then, the embarrassment level went off the charts when we caught him explaining his system to a fellow traveler with a station wagon whom he had just met in the motel parking lot. Of course, with my father being the salesman he was, we saw the man and his family drive away an hour later with *their* spare tire proudly on the luggage rack, their luggage in the trunk and the five of them squeezed in the two front seats. Their kids also looked pained.

But truth be told, they were thinner than we were.

Still, despite cramped, sweaty bodies, the trip was an enormous success. I even grew to like the corny songs that Dad sang and the old songs with lyrics changed to fit the occasion. They were moderately funny and I could tolerate them all...except for one which always left me and Charley looking for an escape route. That would be my father's favorite: *The Dobrusin Song*, sung to the tune of "H-a-double r-i-g-a-n spells Harrigan":

D-o-b-r-u-s-i-n spells Dobrusin
Proud of all the Yiddish blood within me...
No one e'er can say a word agin' me...

Dad loved that song and years later, as his health deteriorated, Mom would try to get him to sing the song over and over again – "Sing the song, Manny" – and worse, sometimes she'd sing it herself.

When she broke into it in the limousine on the way to the cemetery after Dad's funeral, Charley and I looked in vain for a "way back" seat to crawl under.

Besides the songs, my dad had another way to put his imprint on a trip – side trips to sites that no one else wanted to see. One of those spots was the Thomas Jefferson's Serpentine Wall at the University of Virginia. I could not understand why we were there and yawned my way through Dad's lecture on why the wall was famous. But a few months after his death, our family went to Greenfield Village in Dearborn, Michigan and there was a serpentine wall and I remembered just enough of Dad's lecture to bore my kids and leave Ellen an opening to use her usual line: "How do you *know* these things"? Chalk one up for Manny.

Yes, it was a great family trip and Dad never lost his cool the whole time except for three notable occasions.

The first was in York, Pennsylvania. Leaving the Amish farmer's market, I bought a bag of potato chips and opened it while I crossed the street. My father, in utter fear that the potato chips might contain lard screamed out: "WAIT!" causing half the population of York: pedestrians, automobiles, and Amish horse-drawn buggies to stop dead in their tracks. He ran into the street against traffic to rescue me from sin. What dedication!

By the way, they were made with vegetable shortening. I knew that because I had checked before I bought them.

The next time also involved potato chips. (Do I detect a trend here?) We were just checking into another Holiday Inn, this one in Charlottesville, Virginia, when I happened to notice a type of vending machine that I had never seen before. It had an arm behind the glass that swung out and captured a bag of potato chips and dropped them into a slot. I was fascinated by it and ran to tell my brother. At that moment, Dad was struggling with luggage in the 90-degree heat and oppressive humidity, and was neither amused nor interested. He screamed out one of his top ad-libs of all time: "*I take him halfway across the country and all he cares about is a machine that coughs up corn chips.*" Read that line a few times. It has everything: exaggeration, alliteration, simplicity of text. It is a masterpiece. I couldn't possibly capture the intonation, but it has stayed with me forever. I wanted to quote it in the eulogy that I wrote for him but I knew I wouldn't be able to get through it.

The third time was much more subtle. Dad noticed a line at the bottom of a Virginia restaurant menu which said: "We reserve the right to refuse service to anyone we choose." Traveling in the South during that time when civil rights was still in its infancy, such a line shouldn't have been too surprising. But my father made it clear to us back in the car that he was very angry that he hadn't gotten up and left. It bothered him for quite a while.

That was one of the few times I remember my dad saying: "I should have done something." He usually did it, right or wrong and then defended himself if necessary.

If there was ever a man of principle, it was Manny Dobrusin.

Dad passed on the love of travel to me and, thank God, I inherited as well his nearly impeccable sense of direction. It's much easier to travel when you rarely get lost and if you ever do, to justify it by finding something interesting to make the detour worthwhile.

When I reminisce about that trip, I can't help but compare it to the trips Ellen and I and our kids have taken and the long journeys that are part of all of our lives. We have taken the kids to New York City, Toronto, Yellowstone, to the Badlands of South Dakota, to Alaska and to Hawaii, and several times to an undisclosed location in Michigan which we refuse to divulge to anyone lest it become overcrowded. They have all been journeys of discovery and learning and, of course, fun as well. In fact, I like to think that they have been more fun than the trips I took when we were kids because, while my Dad couldn't just let something be fun without an overriding educational message, I have been fortunate to inherit playful genes from my mother's side of the family.

But I also think about the connection between the trips I took as a kid and the ones I have taken as an adult. I think about how those journeys have helped me to prepare for the journeys I take today and how the two are linked.

I rarely traveled alone while the kids were growing up. I much preferred traveling with the family. It's truly the best of both worlds: I have their company of course, but since I plan the trips, they do tend to reflect, even just a bit, my interests. (Serpentine Wall, here we come!)

But every so often each of us needs to travel by ourselves and, in 1999, I took a solo trip that I will never forget. It was a trip that I couldn't share with anyone else and it had a specific connection with the Washington trip of 1966. They are linked by the grave with the Eternal Flame in Arlington National Cemetery that we visited that summer when I was 11.

That moment was special to me because, as we looked at the grave that day, my mother reminded me of a day three years earlier when she had taken me by the hand and walked with me up the street to stand opposite our elementary school. Someone pushed me to the front of the small crowd that had gathered and told me to wave. I waved and I will never forget the smiling face of the man who waved back right at me.

I can still picture it like it was yesterday. He looked right at me. I will forever remember President Kennedy's bright smile as his motorcade sped towards Boston College where he would be delivering an address. Six months later he was assassinated and I, like so many of my age, will never forget that weekend.

So, in 1999, I took a solo journey and I spoke about it the next Yom Kippur:

A JOURNEY OF MEMORY
ROSH HASHANA 1999

Judaism is a religion of text. Jews have elevated text and the analysis of text to a level of unparalleled meaning.

For the Jew, texts have a power all their own, equaled only by the power each of us has to learn from them in our own individual way. Interpreting a text so that it speaks directly about our experience is midrash. The process of making midrash is critical if we are to find meaning in the texts of our lives.

Texts are not only written words. Stories told orally are texts. Music is text.

And...places can be texts.

When a place is important to us, that place becomes the source text for commentaries which can help us to understand our lives more deeply. That is why pilgrimages are so important. When we make a pilgrimage to a holy place, we open ourselves up to that place and it becomes one of the texts for our lives from that point on.

I took a pilgrimage this past year. It was a very meaningful trip in terms of the history I learned. But the pilgrimage surprised me in that, while I thought the trip was about a specific moment and place in time, the lessons I learned were much greater.

I had wanted to go to this place for years. But I had always avoided going. When my Sabbatical presented the opportunity, I couldn't stay away any longer. I summoned up my courage and went on the pilgrimage.

Since a long, arduous journey is an important part of the experience of a pilgrimage, I flew into a city several states away and spent two days driving almost 1,000 miles just to reach the spot.

When I finally arrived at the city of my destination, I checked into a hotel a few blocks away from the pilgrimage site. I began to walk on the streets to Dallas, Texas to the place, Dealey Plaza, and all of the memories flooded back.

I went back in time to that horrible Friday afternoon in November 1963 when President Kennedy was assassinated.

The memories of that weekend are forever etched in my mind. I remember my mother, leaning out the upstairs window informing me with a hesitating voice that she had something to tell me. She was still in a state of shock.

I remember my father shaking when he picked up my grandmother at the movie theater where she had been for several hours. He told her the news and when others started gathering around to ask what had happened, he yelled "I'm not going to be a God damned town crier."

I remember my rabbi crying on the pulpit. I didn't know that rabbis (or any adults for that matter) cried.

I remember walking with the rest of our synagogue community to lay a wreath at President Kennedy's birthplace on Beals Street in Brookline and coming home to watch the film of that procession on the national news.

As the years went by, my interest in the tragedy grew and, since then, I have read so many books, watched so many documentaries, studied the evidence, and heard the theories, and every aspect of the story still fascinates me. So, I needed to go to Dealey Plaza in Dallas to stand in that terrible place.

I knew it would be emotional. But my experience was so different from what I had expected.

Yes, I was fascinated by the historical realities of what happened there. I was intrigued by seeing the exhibits about the assassination and by those who stood at the site eagerly willing to share their conspiracy theories with anyone who wandered by.

But what I didn't expect was that the lessons I learned during the hours I spent at Dealey Plaza were lessons that went far beyond the Kennedy assassination. I was so emotionally connected with Dealey Plaza that it became a text that begged to be interpreted.

As I stood quietly in the Texas sun, I realized there were three verses in this text which were calling out for me: three questions struck me immediately and needed answering.

The first: "**Why does this place seem so much smaller than I thought it would be**?"

The second: "**How can the people of Dallas walk or drive through this place without even stopping to think about where they are?**"

The third: "**How can a crowded place so terribly sad empty into a wide open space, an endless Texas horizon of bright sunshine and blue sky?**"

These were the three questions that struck me after just a few moments at Dealey Plaza and each, upon thought and reflection, yielded a midrash, an interpretation:

Why does this place seem so much smaller than I thought it would be?

The fact is that the assassination of President Kennedy, as tragic as it was, made a greater impact on the lives of many of us than it should have. While it was truly a critical moment in American history and a horrifying moment for those who were personally involved or who witnessed it, I think that the hold this event has over so many of us is less about the event and more about us. We have to look beyond the historical aspect of the event itself and wonder why we make Dealey Plaza so much bigger than it is.

Why are so many people of my age fascinated with the Kennedy assassination? Perhaps it is because it was our first brush with death. Perhaps it is because it was the first time the world didn't make sense to us. Perhaps it is because it was the first time we saw our parents or our teachers cry. Whatever the reason, that small patch of land seems monumental in many minds and I needed to understand why.

When I look at our son approaching the age that I was when JFK was shot, I think I realize a bit better why this event touches me the way it does. It came at an age when I didn't have to think about what the world was all about. Then, suddenly, that world was turned upside down.

I realize how I am so fortunate to be able to say that the event which changed my world was not in my own personal life. I pray my children and all children should be so fortunate. I could watch it as an outsider knowing it really didn't affect me directly.

But the fact remains that the significance and importance of this place is that it was here that I and countless others learned that one horrendous act can end a dream, that sudden sadness is part of life, that the world is not always Camelot.

Because it was such an emotional time, I have never forgotten it. But it is only one place in a world of special places. It isn't as big in real life. This was a place of pilgrimage for me but may not be for others.

And that leads me to my second thought: *"***How can the people of Dallas walk or drive through this place without even stopping to think about where they are?***"*

The events which touch our lives don't always touch others in quite the same way. The citizens of Dallas walk quickly through Dealey Plaza, not to be insensitive to the memory of President Kennedy but because they have their own lives to lead and their own destinations in which to find meaning.

We have to accept the fact that not everyone is on the same journey as we are. We have a right to expect that others will be sensitive to our needs, but we can't expect that everyone see events on the same scale that we do. We can't be so quick to brand others as uncaring or unfeeling when they tread carelessly on our routes of pilgrimage.

We begin a pilgrimage whenever we celebrate a joyous occasion or suffer a tragedy or a loss. We need to know that others care. Jewish tradition places a major emphasis on interpersonal relationships, on being there for others at times of joy and at times of sadness, at the transition times in their lives.

But there must be a limit to our own expectations of others. We have to accept the fact that the time comes for others to move on in their own lives and leave us to finish our pilgrimage on our own, not ignoring us by any means, but leaving us to follow their own itinerary at that moment.

Sometimes we do not show the proper sensitivity to others' journeys and, as a result, don't help them sufficiently along the way. But sometimes we expect too much from others, asking them always to see their world through our eyes, asking them not only to assist us on our pilgrimage but expecting them to travel the same road. That puts too much of a burden on others, especially those closest to us. Others have their own journeys to make. We must let people find their own ways and make their own journeys.

And we too have to suspend our specific journeys on occasion. We have a greater journey through life to take and sometimes our more intense, personal journeys have to take a back seat towards getting through each day and fulfilling our responsibilities in this world.

I learned that vividly as I was leaving Dallas to return to the airport. My route was to take me right through Dealey Plaza and I had spent a significant amount of time pondering how it was going to feel driving over the spot of the assassination. When the time came and I entered the area, a truck suddenly swerved into my lane and by the time I dealt with that sudden intrusion, I had driven past the spot, under the triple underpass and was heading out on the freeway.

All of us have to put aside our spiritual and emotional pilgrimages at times to deal with life as it exists. We might resent the intrusion into our emotional journeys but the fact is, those intrusions can sometimes help us to get our feet back on the ground and resume our bigger pilgrimage through life.

Finally, **How can a crowded place so terribly sad empty into a wide open space, an endless Texas horizon of bright sunshine and blue sky?** Somehow being at Dealey Plaza brought me a strange sense of peace. I walked away from that place feeling differently than when I walked in. I felt that I had faced a place deep within me which needed light. I walked away feeling that something deep within me had been reconciled, not just the need to see this place, but the need to understand my world better.

I kept remembering what I had read about the assassination. Jackie Kennedy had told people that just before the shots rang out, she had looked at the cooling shadow of the overpass ahead and then to the open spaces beyond and had thought how refreshing it would be when they were in that cooling, protective shade and then out of the narrow, confined space.

It is when we experience our deepest sorrows, when we are truly in the narrow places that we need to keep looking for the protection of God's shadow and the brightness of the world which lies ahead.

Sometimes, the narrow crowded places, which seem in our minds to be so overwhelming and so full of people who don't see what we see, block out our abilities to see the sun shining brightly beyond. Let it never be that way. Let us go on our journeys, and, when sadness comes to us or others, let us share our pilgrimages and join with others in theirs as we seek to understand as much of life as we can, but always knowing that God's presence is there to shield us like a cooling shadow and that we will, one day, in this world, in our lifetime, enjoy sunshine and open spaces again.

As I look back on that trip to Dallas, I think how appropriate it was that I took that particular journey alone. There are times when we truly must be alone with our thoughts and our deepest memories. No one else would have understood. Not even my dear family or my closest friends would have felt what I was feeling at that moment.

That leads me to one final thought about my dad: the ultimate family man and active community member. Everything he did, he did for us, and he truly loved to be with us. He believed in unlimited and unending responsibility to family and community.

But unmistakably, he was on his own journey as well. He would sometimes get moody, often retreat into his own world and most always saw things only from his perspective.

A few weeks before he died, Dad was in the hospital and was in significant pain. It was getting towards dinnertime. He told us to go downstairs to the cafeteria and to leave him alone. He wanted to be by himself. He looked so sad and so scared. We were hesitant. But he was stubbornly determined. So we left.

When we came back upstairs, he was humming softly with a smile on his face. I asked him why he was smiling. He looked at me and said words that I will always cherish: "I'm happy. I've been sitting here singing all of my songs."

I shared those words during Dad's funeral and I have never forgotten them.

No matter how much we love those around us and those with whom we share our lives, we sometimes have to sing our own songs and sometimes we have to travel down the roads of life alone. But in the end, we never really travel alone, especially if we share our lessons with others.

2

Just Be Good

My mother, Gertrude Dobrusin, was born in the city of Somerville, Massachusetts, in 1922. She was a New Englander through and through. Her distinctive Boston accent became even more pronounced to my ears after I had largely lost mine and she continued to embrace "Boston lingo" even after most back home had long since stopped using the "old-time" expressions. It was always fun to watch the absolutely clueless look she would receive in Michigan when she asked for the *bubbler*, the classic Bostonian term for "water fountain."

When Mom was a child, her family moved to a farm in the small town of Assinippi, Massachusetts – you can only imagine how much fun we had with that name when we were kids. My mother was not only a born-and-bred New Englander, she was always a farm girl at heart.

Mom's father died when she was in high school and she was tempted to stay home to help her mother with the farm. But my grandmother insisted that she attend college, so Mom commuted to Simmons College in Boston and, after graduation, she worked as a newspaper reporter for *The Quincy Patriot Ledger*, a major Boston area newspaper. She stayed at that job for a few years, giving it up to become engaged to a man she had known for only a few months and went on to live "happily ever after" in every sense of the word.

But Mom must have regretted giving up her career because she remained a reporter throughout her entire life. She was what one might accurately call a newshound. The mere mention of a "breaking story" would leave her breathless and ready to go.

The first vague rumors of a potential snowstorm saw Mom turning on every radio and TV in the house to a different station to monitor all of the reports. When election time came, she was on top of every twist and turn in the campaign. Whatever the story, she was there like a retired race-horse, chomping at the bit to get back onto the track.

Whenever the news bug struck, Dad used to call her "Brenda Starr, Ace Reporter" from the old comic strip. But it wasn't just major stories that would bring out the journalist in her. Often, when she and I would talk, her side of the conversation would take the form of a barrage of questions, one after the other, as she tried to get all the facts and find "the story behind the story."

After I became a rabbi, I would always call home on Saturday nights and we had essentially the same conversation every week:

Me: "Hi, Mom."
Mom: "Hi, how were services today?"
Me: "Fine."
Mom: "Did you get a crowd?"
Me: "Yes."
Mom: "Did they like your sermon?"
Me: "Yes."
Mom: "Did anyone criticize you?"
Me: "No." (Of course someone usually did but telling her would have been a grave mistake.)

All the while, she would be deflecting questions I asked her, preferring instead to be the objective reporter whose job it was to find out about everyone else while not revealing her own opinions.

Perhaps that explains a strange revelation that came over me while we flew together from Boston to Ann Arbor in June 2002. Dad had died the year before and Mom was moving to Michigan to be closer to us. We were both heading into uncharted territory, and as I looked at her sleeping in the seat next to me, two thoughts came to mind. First, I sensed that the parent and child roles had switched the moment the plane left the ground. And second, I realized that, while I certainly loved and admired her, I wasn't sure I ever really knew her completely. There was always an aura of mystery around her and I think that's how she wanted it.

It took me until a moment 35,000 feet over Ohio in my forty-seventh year to finally confront this fact, but looking back, I think I had known about her mysterious side for years. This was mostly because of what Charley and I called: "*The Face.*"

Some people have become famous for one particular facial expression (Lucy Ricardo's "eewww" face comes to mind) and, while it didn't achieve great fame for her, Mom had a look, unique to her: an inscrutable combination of pride, uncertainty, discomfort, satisfaction, and joy mixed with her trademark humility and reticence to show deep emotion. This look is impossible to describe adequately, but we experienced it often and could anticipate its appearance during any significant moment of family life.

Not only could you see "The Face," but you could hear it over the phone too. When I was studying in Israel for a year, Mom would send me letters and I could read "The Face" two or three times in each letter.

I wish I had understood "The Face" better. I honestly wish I had understood her better than I did.

Still, some things were very clear: my mother was quite simply a supremely kind, gentle woman with an infectious smile. She loved my father with all of her heart and defended and protected him from a world occasionally cruel. She loved my brother and I deeply and had her own way of dealing with life's major quandaries with comments which often left my father howling with laughter and left us all scratching our heads.

For example, one day, Mom told me on the phone that she had gone to a synagogue in a nearby town for services. Like our home synagogue, it was a Conservative one. Unlike ours, this congregation used a newer version of the prayer book.

This time I played the part of the reporter and repeatedly asked her how she liked the new book. Finally, she said that she didn't like it at all. So I pressed a bit (always a bit dangerous with Mom), asking her why she didn't like it. Her answer was vintage Gert Dobrusin: "I didn't like the tunes."

This answer tells a lot about her. Things had their own way of fitting together for Mom and it didn't matter if the rest of us didn't see it in the same way. Mom moved to her own music.

She had her own theology as well.

Once, when I was about 13, I yelled at her about something. I turned away and stubbed my toe pretty badly. Mom said, as she always did at times like this: "There, you see, God punished you." With a nascent interest in spiritual matters, I yelled back: "Do you really believe that?"

My mother paused for a moment and then answered: "Not really... But still, God punished you."

It wasn't until years later that I appreciated how brilliant my mother's retort was. Of course, we say we believe in God and I assume most of us who say so really do. But when pressed, we are likely to admit that there is often a disconnect between what we say we believe and what we believe in reality.

Inconsistent theology aside, my mother was a deeply religious person and a deeply spiritual person, but not in any of the ways that often count for religiosity or spirituality among most serious Jews today. She really didn't like going to synagogue unless it was to watch me conduct services and she always would find a good and righteous excuse to stay home if she could. She was always a bit uncomfortable performing rituals and would always put on "The Face" when she lit Shabbat candles, especially if someone was watching.

Then there was Christmas.

I assume that my brother and I are among the few rabbis who are Jews by birth who diligently hung stockings up next to the fireplace every Christmas Eve. My mother could not bear to imagine that we would think we had been bad boys because Santa didn't come to us. So, until we were 5 or 6, stockings went up – no tree, God forbid – strudel or mandel bread was put out on the table for St. Nick and we went to bed knowing there would be presents in the morning. When I transferred our old 8mm home movies to DVD, I considered deleting the scenes of opening presents on Christmas morning but I decided to leave them in. I am so glad that I did.

While we stopped putting stockings up, Mom still fiercely believed that there was nothing wrong with her singing Christmas carols at home and even told me I was "bigoted" (I asked Dad what that meant and he told me to look it up) for not wanting to sing *The First Noel* with my 6th grade class at the public school Christmas assembly. I did end up singing and survived the entire ordeal. Actually, I enjoyed it and that pleased my mother tremendously.

She was happy that we found such meaning in Jewish ritual even if it didn't really resonate with her. But after we were grown and left the house, she began to meditate each day. At least that's what she called her practice of going back to bed for an hour after breakfast. She called it her "meditation time" and despite the fact that she probably was the only person in the world who meditated with the morning news blaring on the radio, she kept up the routine for years and used to tell everyone that she meditated.

Even given the lack of commitment to Jewish observance and her unorthodox meditation style, Mom was, in one sense, one of the most spiritual people I have ever known. Her beliefs shaped me and continue to shape my views on life in general.

I say this because she believed so deeply in being good and never did anything to purposefully hurt anyone, even to her own detriment. She was always so obsessed with the concern that others might think poorly of us that she would push us to go the extra mile to do things for others: "It would mean the world to them" she would say when urging us to call family members. "But were they mad at you?" she would ask us if we stood up for ourselves in certain situations. Being good and being liked was all that mattered to her.

In that spirit, let me offer a sermon that I delivered on Yom Kippur a few years back, shortly after Mom died. It was part of a series of four sermons which was based on four wishes we express during the *mishebayrach* prayer that we say for a bar or bat mitzvah.

One of the things that we hope for our children is that "they walk in God's ways." The sermon came from my heart and they were my words but, in retrospect, I have to say that the thought came from Mom.

WALKING IN GOD'S WAYS
YOM KIPPUR 2005

You might remember the television show called The Paper Chase. Each week, during the opening credits, we would hear John Houseman, who played Professor Kingsfield, speak about the challenges of law school. He would end by saying in his inimitable style: "You come in with a skull full of mush and – if you survive – you leave thinking like a lawyer."

I don't know if my skull was full of mush when I entered rabbinical school, but in one critical way I did leave thinking like a pulpit rabbi. Since the moment I received my diploma, I have not been able to watch a TV show or a movie, listen to a song, or read a newspaper without thinking of a potential sermon. All rabbis think like this but as I look back on my sermons of the past, I realize I probably act on those thoughts more than most of my colleagues.

I must have begun thinking like a rabbi right away – the first movie I saw after ordination was E.T. and I immediately began to compose my first High Holy Day sermon on the way home from the movie theatre. At the end of the film, E.T. says good-bye to his friend Elliot by pointing to the boy's head and saying: "I'll be right here." When I heard those words, my mind began racing about their implications: How do we keep God "right here"? How do we capture the spirit of Mt. Sinai when we stood together with God? These words represented to me God's invitation to us to remain connected with the Divine through our actions and our faith.

Looking back on it, I started thinking like a rabbi a moment later than I should have, because E.T. said something even more important just before he said: "I'll be right here," and it wasn't until I sat down to watch the movie with my kids many years later that I realized it.

As a "rookie" rabbi, I probably would have thought that this earlier line was too simple a statement to serve as the basis for a sermon. But if my years in the rabbinate have taught me anything, it is to have more faith in simple statements, and so this sermon is based on other, simpler words of E.T.

Just before he said goodbye to Elliot, E.T. said to 6-year-old Gertie: "Be good."

That's all: "Be good."

There is no more basic and no more important statement than this.

When I think about the B'nai and B'not mitzvah standing on the bima, I sometimes feel I should grab each of them, look them in the eye, and say: "Be good." Even if they decide not to obligate themselves to observing the commandments, even if they don't think about God in their lives, even if they never open a book of Jewish wisdom…even so, if they follow the advice: "Be Good" and connect it with being a Jew, somehow I feel that, in one important way, we and they will have done enough.

Of course, it's not enough. Judaism is too multifaceted to be encapsulated by the expectation to be a good person. But being good is the sine qua non; it is the absolute and only thing that ultimately matters.

One can find many Jewish philosophers and thinkers who believe differently. To some, Judaism is not to be seen as a tool for either personal or universal good. It is simply a faith based on doing the commandments for their own sake and ensuring our future as a distinct people. I reject that idea. It makes no sense to me. None of this makes any sense to me unless it leads us to "be good."

Now, if I wanted to say: "Be good" in Hebrew, I'd have a difficult time. There really is no exact Hebrew equivalent for that simple phrase.

But there are ways to tell people to do good things. One way is to say: "Lech bidarchay Eloheem," "Walk in God's ways."

In the traditional prayer for a bar or bat mitzvah, we express several wishes: that he or she be wholehearted in faith, observe the commandments, and study Torah. But we also express the wish that the bar or bat mitzvah will walk in God's ways.

The traditional texts explain this somewhat vague concept rather clearly. In one text we read: "These are the ways of the Holy One: God is gracious and compassionate, patient, abounding in kindness and faithfulness. Just as God is gracious and compassionate, you too must be gracious and compassionate. As God is faithful, you too must be faithful. As God is loving, you too must be loving."

In a related text in the Talmudic tractate of Sotah, we read that Rabbi Hama said in the name of Rabbi Hanina: "What does it mean to follow God? The verse means to teach us that we should follow the attributes of the Holy One, in clothing the naked, visiting the sick, comforting the bereaved."

This is what it means to tell our children to walk in God's ways: "In your attitude and in your actions, may you be good."

That "being good" is of central importance in Judaism can be seen from the haftarah, the reading of the Prophets, chosen for Yom Kippur morning. This haftarah includes the prophet Isaiah's impassioned plea that we not only fast but that we also share our bread with the hungry, let the oppressed go free, clothe the naked, and defeat wickedness. At the high point of the Jewish year, the message of the prophet is simply: "Be good and do good."

But it is not easy. It never has been and Isaiah knew it.

The haftarah begins with the following words; The Lord says: "Build up, build up a highway! Clear a road! Remove all obstacles from the road of my people."

There are obstacles to walking on the path of goodness and we all know them very well. It's hard to be good. It is easier to be selfish and insensitive than to truly care for others. It takes time and energy to reach beyond our own immediate needs.

And, it is frustrating as well. We know that the road to hell is paved with good intentions and no good deed goes unpunished and we don't always get what we deserve. So, it is hard to convince our young people and to convince ourselves that goodness is, in fact, often its own reward.

But we continue to try.

And as we try, we should recognize there are two other obstacles to being good.

The first is taught to us in one of the most beautiful and eternal verses in the entire Tanach. The prophet Micah teaches that what God wants from us is: "to do justice, love mercy and walk humbly with God."

The key word is walking "humbly" with God. If you want to walk in God's ways, says Micah, you must be humble. One of the major obstacles to being good is the arrogance that comes from believing that each of us knows exactly what is "good."

There is a temptation to believe that the good path in any given situation is so clear and self-evident that there is no room for debate. Often this is true. But many times it is not true and we have page after page after page of Talmudic debate to prove it. To decide what is God-like and good is not easy much of the time, and one of the greatest obstacles to being good occurs when we surround ourselves only with like-thinking people, discredit those on "the other side," and determine that we and those around us have the only ultimate answer.

It can't be that way. While we may easily recognize evil when we see it, finding the truly good course of action is not as easy. In Judaism, knowing the good comes from deep thought and consideration, trial and error, listening to various opinions when they are expressed respectfully with consideration for that which you hold most dear. We must evaluate different ideas and never believe that we have found the ultimate path, for with complacency comes arrogance and with arrogance good is impossible to achieve.

Our children cannot and must not be told that one side or the other – whether blue states or red states, old or young, or any such pair of opposites – has the monopoly on truth. The struggle of opposing ideas, opinions, and priorities must continue throughout the course of our lives. Eventually, we hope for our children to feel comfortable with their identities and find their place in this world of infinite perspectives. And this is good, because too much discussion and evaluation can be paralyzing. But if we ever close ourselves or our children off to other opinions, believing that our answers are the only answers, we are no longer walking humbly along the path. So we must keep our minds open and, while we should find the place on spectrums that we feel comfortable with, we should never stop listening to voices on all sides and must remain open to learning from others.

Then there is a second obstacle to being good. The Torah teaches: "It is not good for a human being to be alone." Let me turn the sentence around: "A human being cannot be good alone."

From the Jewish perspective, isolation is another significant obstacle to being good. It is impossible to be good acting alone.

So we form relationships with loved ones to create a home and with those who share our values to form community. Then we reach beyond to truly work with others to help make this a good world. It is only in community that we can "be good" and the major purpose of a community in Jewish life is to do good things together.

During the Exodus, Moses sends 12 spies to scout out the land of Canaan and return with information about the land. They all come back and say that the land is beautiful, but 10 of the 12 banded together and said: "We can't conquer it, the people there are too strong." Their message becomes more and more negative in the face of staunch loyalty from the two faithful spies Caleb and Joshua, until finally the ten encourage the people to return to Egypt.

And the people cried that night in their tents and wanted to return to Egypt.

The community had banded together for a negative purpose. God punishes them by telling them that their generation will die in the desert never reaching the Promised Land.

What is our response to God? Our response for 2,000 years has been to gather as a community, minimally of 10, a minyan, 10 to balance out the disloyal and destructive acts of each of those 10 spies and to say to God: "We can do better as a community. We can, in fact, produce good instead of bad. We can fulfill our responsibilities. We can stay on the path you have ordained for us, not try to turn back or go in a different direction. We can reach the Promised Land."

We must gather a minyan around us because it does take a village to do good.

Being good alone is as impossible as it is meaningless. "Acting good" with the support and the strength of community means everything. And that goes across religious lines as well.

We cannot do good alone. We need to continue to seek out those of all faiths who truly wish for good in the world who can teach us and whom we can teach, who can inspire us and whom we can inspire, who can influence us and whom we can influence by joining hands together to help make this a better world.

So, let us pledge to remove the obstacles that prevent us from walking in God's path. Let us pledge to listen more carefully, jump to conclusions less often, be a little less dogmatic. And always, always understand that in community, narrowly and widely defined, we can better reach our goals.

We must all seek to walk in God's ways. We must all "be good." For in the end, that is all that matters.

That one was for Mom.

She was obsessed with the idea of being good. It motivated her and it drove her through her life.

She was also in love with the beauty of the natural world.

Mom often told me: "I find my religion in the flowers and the trees." And while she was hardly what one would call an outdoorswoman, she loved to look at nature from comfortable places inside the house or the car.

She had her own ritual as each spring she would take us to the window every day and show us the buds on the trees, which I imagine was her equivalent of witnessing the giving of the Torah at Mt. Sinai. She would look at them with tears in her eyes and loved that moment deeply.

She also loved animals although we never had one in our house, except for the turtle that sadly met his fate when a sudden New

England cold snap struck and left him frozen on the porch. But when she talked of her days on the farm and reminisced about Dukie the dog, Goo-Goo the duck, and the pigs and the chickens, she would smile so happily. When she would visit us in Ann Arbor, she absolutely loved the animals who share our home who were drawn to her in some magical way as well.

Through it all, the most important sign of my mother's spirituality was that she was a dreamer and an absolute, undaunted optimist. To her, as my brother said in his eulogy at her funeral, "The glass wasn't only half full, it was all full."

"Everything will be okay," she would say, no matter what the situation.

Late in life, she suffered a terribly unfair twist of fate. After years of taking care of her children, her mother, and then my dad, she moved out to live near us to spend time with her grandchildren and to enjoy her remaining years. Shortly after she came, she developed a terribly painful and debilitating disease which severely limited her.

Still, she took it all in stride.

And she never complained.

Her journey through this life was, despite being enigmatic at times, a joy to behold. Her belief in the goodness of people continues to be a foundation of my practice as a Jew.

Her sense of Torah was not the one that I have chosen. But her search for holiness in her own way guided me in my choice of career and, more importantly, in my search for meaning in the world we live in.

Speaking of Torah, my mother didn't have much interest in studying traditional texts. But she found wisdom in other places. One of those was in the words of Charlie Brown and the whole Peanuts gang and she probably considered this her "Torah" as much as anything else. I think she was onto something very important. To close this chapter then, let me share a sermon I delivered about Peanuts as a tribute to my mother, whose example still shines for me and for so many who knew her.

WISDOM FROM THE COMICS
2006

The source for my remarks today is not the Torah. But it has earned its own standing for me as a critical source of learning. For decades it has been a font of wisdom, insight, and meaning and will remain, I am sure, a source of learning and joy for generations to come.

The source features situations to which we can all relate, introduces us to characters with whom we can all identify, showcases the talents and the weaknesses of human beings we all know, and always seems so perceptively to reflect the reality of our struggles to make sense out of our world.

We know the characters so well for they resemble us. Like us, they populate a world which at once is too big for them and yet which is just the right size. That they are children reminds us of our subservience to a presence greater than us. That they are in a world without visible adults reminds us that we decide our own destiny and cannot directly see that presence. We must depend on ourselves and on our own limited intelligence and experience to make sense of a world which is so rapidly changing around us as we grow.

And we owe all of this insight to one man, one genius who, by sharing his talent with the world and displaying his soul so publicly, changed all of our lives. This man's name was Charles Schulz.

I don't imagine there is anyone who can honestly say: "I don't like Peanuts." Other art forms are more dramatic and more brilliant, but our world has never been the same since Charlie Brown came on the scene.

While I could go on for hours about my favorite Peanuts strips, I will share with you only one gem: my favorite Charlie Brown cartoon.

Charlie Brown, Linus, and Lucy are lying on their backs looking up into the sky and Lucy asks the others to tell her what they see in the cloud formations.

Linus talks about the clouds looking like a map of British Honduras, the profile of a noted sculptor and "the stoning of Stephen ... I can see the apostle Paul standing there to one side."

And Lucy says: "Uh huh, that's very good. What do YOU see in the clouds, Charlie Brown?"

And Charlie Brown says: "Well, I was going to say I saw a ducky and a horsey but I changed my mind."

Charlie Brown's answer at first seems so sad. You can't but feel pity for him. He feels completely out of his league.

But then we notice something. Charlie Brown isn't "thinking" this. He is **saying** it. He might have "changed his mind" but he said it anyway. I don't think this is a sign of his well-documented "wishy-washiness." Rather, I think it is a brilliant statement: "I was going to say it but changed my mind but I honestly think you need to hear it anyway." He looked at a younger friend who had seized the moment and impressed everyone with all that he knew and Charlie Brown still said his simple piece and I love him for it.

We need to think deeply about Judaism. Our Judaism needs to grow as we grow. We need, to the best of our ability, to look at the forms around us and utter statements of wisdom, linking events of today to those in the past, rattling off the names and ideas of the Jewish philosophers and artists, the thinkers and the poets, and relate them to that which swirls around us. We need to look up into the sky and understand the wisdom of the ages.

But we need as well to remember that the wisdom of the ages is sometimes found in the simple stirrings of the human heart, in seeing the duckies and the horsies around us and not being afraid to say so. Wisdom can be found in seeing this world with childlike eyes no matter how old those eyes might be, in seeing and being satisfied with simple answers to complex questions, relating to a Judaism of the heart and the childlike wonder and joy of the world.

Sometimes, I fear, in our zeal to bring great meaning to our Judaism, we make it too difficult. Others often raise the bar so high that we are not comfortable responding, feeling that what we can add is not appreciated and not valued. Like Charlie Brown, we may feel like we should change our minds about saying what we feel. Unlike him, we may in fact swallow our words and remain silent.

But we deprive ourselves when we do this. For the answers to our deepest questions as Jews, and as human beings, are often to be found in the simplest words and in the simplest, purest meaning. Those ideas can be voiced by anyone, no matter how much or how little they know about the intricacies of our faith, the language of our people, the words of ancient rabbis, or the current sociological theories.

May we always continue our serious investigation of all that Judaism is and all that it can be. May we struggle with Torah and grapple with ideas. May we fret or, God willing, rejoice over population studies and look for new spiritual awakenings. May we make great plans for ensuring our people's future and bringing meaning to a new generation of Jews.

May we also find plenty of time to lie on our backs in the cool grass, look up into the sky and see the simplest of visions and then have the confidence to share them with others.

As we look for role models around us, let us learn from those whose examples shine for us in our contemporary world as well as those who came before us. And let us always look for role models in unexpected places.

And so let us learn.

From Schroeder, who played the most beautiful piano music with his talented hands on a toy piano, let us learn to take the simple instruments we have: our hands, our voices, our hearts, and make the most beautiful music, rising above all of our limitations to make the best use of the talents we have been given.

From Linus, who carried his security blanket everywhere, let us learn to treasure the things which bring us security in the world: holding tight to family, friends, and faith to help us steer our way through the difficult days ahead.

From Lucy, who showed brash chutzpah, let us learn to face this world with confidence but let us figure out a way to leave the arrogance behind and make room for others and respect them.

From Pig Pen, who perpetually walked in a cloud of dust, let us really be a part of this world, let us get dirty helping others, let us feel the earth *between our fingers and our toes, and let us rejoice in a love of the world we live in.*

From Charlie Brown, who always came back for more, let us learn to trust even if we get hurt on occasion, learn to dream even if the rest of the world laughs, and learn to get back on the pitcher's mound again even after we get hit so hard that it knocks us over.

Finally, from Snoopy, let us love our homes, let us love our meals, and let us always dance with joy and always, always let us dream great things.

The more I think of it, Peanuts is definitely a form of Torah and the more I think of it, my mother might have had a kindred spirit in Snoopy.

I'll take the risk that some might think I'm demeaning my mother with this comparison. Believe me, I'm not. My mother would have been proud of it. After all, she was a dreamer, a loyal and loving companion to my dad and to all of us, so full of positive energy and so full of joy. Maybe I know enough about her after all.

Maybe that's all any of us need to know and need to be.

May her memory be for a blessing. Believe me, it is.

3

Imagining A Perfect World

From the outside, our two-family house was similar to so many others in the Brighton neighborhood of Boston. The house was built in the early part of the 20th century. Windows faced onto the quiet tree-lined street and the short steps and small porch in the front of the house were perfect for summer evenings of chatting with the neighbors. For some reason, our front porch was the gathering place. The neighbors would bring folding lawn chairs and everyone would sit and catch up on each other's lives.

Meanwhile, the kids would play Wiffle Ball or touch football in the middle of the street with only an occasional shout of "Car!" and a scramble to safety interrupting the game.

It was a picture of a simpler, quieter time, and each house, each family, seemed so much the same.

But our house was unique in one way. While it was a two-family house, it really was a one family home as everyone at the reddish brown house on Radnor Road was part of the same extended family.

My uncle and aunt and cousins lived downstairs and we lived upstairs with the matriarch of the family, my grandmother, Nana Belle.

Living with my grandmother gave my brother and me many opportunities to realize the holiness of the obligation to respect and honor our elders.

Living with my grandmother also gave us a lot of laughs – mostly, I must admit after all these years, at her expense.

Nana took fine care of us when our parents were away. She was a fantastic cook and an inspiring, hard working, and impressive woman. But her greatest legacy for us was that she unintentionally provided us with great comedic material.

Her comments on baseball: "*Why doesn't that one throw it so the other one can hit it?*"; on football: "*That man fell down and they're still pushing each other!*"; or at my brother's first attempts, after a year in Israel, to introduce the family to Middle Eastern food: "*I'll have an egg,*" accompanied by her patented act of drumming of fingers on the table will all be remembered forever.

But echoing loudest of all is her signature line, a line which she used every time we disappointed her or failed to see something her way. Nana would assume a stern expression, stare at us, and say simply: "*Too damn bad about you.*"

We heard that one a lot.

My grandmother's spaghetti and meatballs, beef stew, and apple pie were the stuff of legends. Equally memorable were her Yiddish expressions, some of which were either made up or, with English thrown in, had become somewhat unintelligible to a serious Yiddish speaker and which, when recalled more than 25 years after her death, still can make my kids laugh hysterically.

Then, there was the ritual of Nana's twice-weekly penny poker game which rotated around several nearby homes. When it was at our house, we always wanted to be there for the fun, especially in the years when the eyesight of most of the players had started to worsen and there was constant and unabashed "guessing" going on. Everyone just trusted each other and the games took on a surrealistic air as no one dared question what cards players said they held in their hands.

But the highlight of our days with Nana Belle was unquestionably the annual visits to the family cemetery plots scattered around Greater Boston. We would pile into the car just before Rosh Hashanah and waited for the fun.

On the way, Nana would regale us with stories about the long trolley trips to the cemetery that she took when she was a kid. She told us that her family would bring a huge picnic lunch which they would eat on the cemetery grounds between crying spells.

Then, as we approached the cemeteries, she would review for us the secret stories of the family, stories which got progressively more complete as we got older, but that, even when we were in our 20s, ended just short of the best parts.

When she would go to the graves, Nana would talk directly to the people buried there: *"See, your grandson said this prayer, he's going to be a rabbi, so it counts."* Or, even better: *"You were always such a good friend"* until we were out of earshot from the grave whereupon she would resume ranting and raving about her "good friend's" laziness and worthlessness.

It was a great family outing. All we needed to recapture the glory of the past generations was time to relax on the grass with a picnic lunch like the old days. I actually suggested that once and received a *"too damn bad about you"* from Nana, who preferred stopping for a fancy dinner on the way home to try to balance out the intense psychological trauma of visiting the graves of cousins who had been dead for more than 30 years.

My grandmother's life had taken some unexpected turns for a woman who came here on "the boat" from Russia when she was 6 months old. When a doctor urged my grandfather to get out of the city to the more relaxing pace in the country, he bought some land and started "Belle's Farm," a fruit and vegetable market which later added a gas station and a "tea room." Nana's stories of the farm were legendary; and when we watched my uncle's home movies taken in the 1930s, we actually got to see the family farm in action.

There was my grandfather who died years before I was born, smiling at the camera and playfully poking a customer with an ear of corn. There was my mother, who always said that this was the happiest time of her life, in work shoes, white socks, and a simple dress standing in front of bushels of vegetables. There was my grandmother standing proudly over the whole operation while preparing the chickens for her famous "Roast Duck" sandwiches. (That's an old family joke.)

We drove by the site of the farm many times when we were kids, but Mom and Nana never wanted to stop and look around. They cherished the memory of those days and weren't prepared to enter the rather ordinary motel which had replaced their home.

But shortly after Mom died, I took Mickie on a trip to Boston and we stopped in Assinippi so she could do some research for a family history report she had to write. With a little bit of investigative work, we were able to find a woman whose husband had worked for Nana in the 1940s and remembered the family perfectly.

She was overjoyed to meet us and thrilled to see Mickie whom she correctly said looked just like my mother. She then proceeded to confirm every story we had heard, right down to the one about Dukie, the family dog and his habit of sleeping in the middle of the street until the police would come over and wake him up gently, telling him to go home. These weren't just rural legends. They were true history.

This was the history of the only Jewish family in Assinippi, Massachusetts; and for all of the jokes, I realized what chutzpah Nana had. She had run a nominally traditional Jewish home in the middle of a small New England country town. She continued to operate the farm for years after my grandfather died. After this, she moved to Boston and eventually took a job selling dresses at the Jordan Marsh Department Store, continually lying about her age until her failing eyesight forced her to retire well into her 70s.

She was quite a force in our family and the five of us shared our lives. We also shared one bathroom and how we pulled that off, God only knows. It was a loving home, no doubt, but, truthfully, despite my father's dramatic outbursts and my grandmother's shtick, it was more ordinary than anything else. All it needed was a little excitement.

I managed to find that excitement someplace and it started with one chance encounter with Nana.

I have a vivid memory of that day when I was 5 or 6 years old. I can still picture myself wandering into the room where she was watching TV. I asked her what she was watching and she said one word:

"Lucy."

I had never heard that word before but I looked at the TV and I can, to this day, remember exactly what I saw. Lucy Ricardo was pushing her way into a card game with Ricky and Fred and their friends. She pretended she knew how to play and then she tried to shuffle the cards and ended up scattering them all over the table and all over Ricky.

I can still hear Nana saying: *"That Lucy is a card."*

I didn't know what that meant. But it didn't matter.

I took one look at Lucy's wild eyes and that expressive face and *I was in love.*

I loved to laugh when I was a kid and Lucy could make me laugh like no one else.

Lucy dressed like Carmen Miranda, lip-synching to a record that suddenly speeds up uncontrollably; Lucy tripping a waiter with a pie landing on the actor William Holden whom I had never heard of but it didn't matter; Lucy stomping grapes in Italy; Lucy with a loving cup stuck to her head trying to be inconspicuous on the subway by pretending to read a paper; Lucy hawking *Vitametavegamin* while steadily becoming drunk. I loved them all and knew the dialogues by heart. And whenever I would watch them, my father would look at me and say: "Again? What a waste of time!" I knew Dad was right. It was time to find other interests.

So, I found Rob and Laura Petrie, Ralph and Alice Kramden, Ed and Trixie Norton, the Cleavers and Andy and Barney, and later, the Bunkers and Oscar and Felix. Each of them holds a special place in my heart. Such a special place it is that at our wedding reception, a close friend toasted us by expressing the hope that our lives would be as adventurous as the Ricardos, as peaceful as the Cleavers, as funny as the Kramdens.

I still love these shows. I have episode after episode on my bookshelf in my study and I watch them over and over and try to get my kids to overlook the fact that they are in black and white to find the real treasure. I use them to supplement my teaching when they will help pass along a message and even sometimes when they don't.

There is something about situation comedies, the good and the bad, which touches our hearts as Americans. Still, I was always a bit reticent to admit my love of sitcoms to any but my closest friends until one Rosh Hashanah. I decided to speak that day on the most significant classic situation comedy quotations for Jews to know. I expected some laughter, most of it incredulous. I got more than I could have hoped for, most of it sincere.

I certainly didn't expect the numbers of otherwise normal, intelligent, reasonably sane people who came up to me afterwards with some of the most animated reactions I ever received to a sermon: "Why didn't you mention Seinfeld?" "Why didn't you give the other famous quote from the All in the Family episode you mentioned?" "How could you quote Ricky Ricardo without using a Cuban accent?" "What makes you say that Ralph and Alice Kramden really loved each other so much?" "Why did you ignore Buddy Sorrel when you quoted from Dick Van Dyke?"

It was then that I realized that most Americans of a certain age have a clandestine love affair with the Ricardos and the Petries and the Cleavers. So now I admit it proudly: I love classic sitcoms.

I also love classic game shows too, but one confession at a time.

When these shows were first produced, most of them represented a vision of what Americans dreamed of for themselves. We longed to wear pearls and suits to breakfast and envisioned our homes as a place where the problems were minor, touched with humor, and solved within half an hour. That place really exists, for so many of us, in Mayfield and Mayberry.

And our entire world can be Mayberry if we make it so.

So here, in that spirit and in memory of Nana Belle who probably would have made a great sitcom character in her own right, is my sermon from that Rosh Hashanah morning which might or might not have changed the way my congregants thought of TV, but certainly changed the way they thought about me.

BRINGING THE MESSIAH—IN HALF AN HOUR
Rosh Hashana 1996

Today I want to present to you an authentically Jewish, challenging, and compelling way of working for the redemption of our world. I want to address on an individual level what each of us can do to bring the Messiah or the Messianic era or Tikkun Olam or whatever you choose to call it.

Whatever you call it, we must believe in it. We must believe in this story. We must believe the world can and will be better, and we must believe that you and I and everyone in the world can make that happen. Perhaps it is a myth. But no myth deserves greater attention, greater dedication, and greater affirmation.

Today, I want to offer you five things that you can do to help bring redemption to the world. They are all derived from the same unexpected source. They are derived from the world of classic TV situation comedies.

Why sitcoms? Simply because most classic TV sitcoms were often based on a vision of perfection, an idyllic place where parents and children got along so well, where people never lost their jobs permanently or faced serious health crises, where problems could always be solved in 22 minutes (allowing for commercials). If this isn't a vision of the Messianic era, nothing is.

So let's talk about bringing the Messiah.

My first quotation comes from the most beloved anti-hero in situation comedy in history: that great philosopher Archie Bunker.

In one episode of All in the Family, Edith, Archie's naive wife, answers an ad in a magazine to set up what she thinks is a casual friendship with another couple, only to find out that a simple friendly relationship wasn't exactly what the other couple had in mind. Edith hadn't realized the meaning of the word "swingers" in the ad.

The couple shows up at the Bunker home and, while the visit begins innocently enough, it quickly turns into total chaos as this decidedly "modern" couple threatens every social value Archie ever dreamed of. Finally, he ushers them out of the house and the chaos is ended. Peace and quiet has returned to the simple Bunker home. Then Archie turns to Edith and with the most wonderful comic pause and the whole world waiting for his chastising of his innocent wife, he says very quietly and firmly: "Don't you read no more magazines!" Edith nods meekly.

The first rule for bringing redemption to the world is "Don't listen to him." In fact don't listen to anyone who tells you that the secret of avoiding the chaos of the world is to bury yourself in a closed world in which there is no exposure to new ideas, in which learning and reading and studying and experiencing this world is off limits. Yes, we need to be careful what we expose ourselves and our children to. But bringing the Messiah is not just a matter of shaping our own personal religious lives, not only about our observing unique ritual commandments while closing off the world. We will bring the Messiah not through building walls to close the world out, but by seeing what the outside world can offer, making appropriate choices and developing our minds as well as our souls.

The second quotation comes from everyone's favorite: I Love Lucy. In this scene, Lucy and Ethel have promised not to gossip and have made a bet with their husbands as to who can refrain from gossiping the longest. In one scene, the two women are standing in the living room where they think they are out of earshot of their husbands when they start sharing gossip. However, the husbands are, in fact, in the basement listening through the furnace pipes.

Suddenly, we hear Fred Mertz, Ethel's husband, speaking from the basement: "Ethel Mertz, this is your conscience, you've been gossiping." Lucy turns to Ethel and says: "Ethel, you've got the loudest conscience I've ever heard."

Then we hear Ricky, Lucy's Cuban husband, say in his trademark accent: "Lucy Ricardo, this is your conscience, you've been gossipin'." Lucy says to Ethel: "Oh fine, my conscience has an accent."

There it is. The next way to bring the Messiah: Develop a loud conscience with an accent.

We need to train ourselves and to teach our children to have a loud Jewish conscience. We need to remember that how we act in any given situation ought to be consistent with the highest ideals and values of our tradition. This isn't to say that other traditions do not have as valuable a conscience – of course they do. But conscience has to be grounded in something and ours ought to be grounded in our Jewish values.

I believe that the Messianic age will be one in which the best of each religious, ethnic, cultural, and educational tradition will somehow produce a world in which we can each continue to follow our own traditions in harmony and security. It will only happen when each of the world's peoples develops a loud conscience with its own personal accent.

Be part of it. Lead the world in the right direction.

Now, to the Dick Van Dyke Show. I can't leave that favorite out. Laura Petrie, while appearing as a contestant on a network game show, has just inadvertently revealed a secret, telling a nation of TV watchers that her husband's boss, TV star Alan Brady, is bald and wears a toupee.

Of course, Alan Brady, played by Carl Reiner is furious. Laura comes to his office to try to make peace. She tells him: "I always liked you better bald." He says: "If this is so, why didn't you tell me?" She says: "I didn't think it was my place." He screams: "No, your place is on network television."

Message #3: Find your place. Each of us has a stage in this drama of bringing in the Messianic era. Find yours. It may be on a very visible local or national stage in which what you do sends a message to thousands and lives on forever as a legacy to untold numbers of generations.

But you may also be the person who rescues injured animals or teaches children how to read or brings food to a hungry person or who returns a lost object. Find your stage and play your part to the best of your ability.

There is a beautiful statement in the Talmud: "There are those who earn their place in the world to come over a lifetime and those who do so in one hour." There are those who play their part in front of everyone throughout their lives, and those who do one thing at one moment or little things consistently over a period of time which change this world piece by piece by piece. Find your stage and play your part.

Now, I want to move on to one of my other favorite shows: "The Honeymooners." Many dislike this show because of Ralph Kramden's verbal abuse of his wife Alice. It is atrocious. It is difficult to listen to and it is sometimes difficult for me to laugh at his threats to his wife. What is especially sad, though, is that it is evident how much he loves her and respects her; and it tears your heart out to think that he can't control his obviously exaggerated and never-acted-upon threats to send her to the moon.

But setting that aside for a moment, the show is a classic. In one scene Ralph thinks he is going to try to win a fortune on a TV game show. Alice is trying to keep him from risking too much. She'd be happy with much less in winnings at much less risk. He stomps around the old dilapidated apartment with its second hand furniture and says; "No, I'm going the whole way. Next week at this time, we'll be living on Park Avenue." And then he says; "And just wait till you see how this furniture looks in a Park Avenue apartment."

Maimonides warned us not to think the world was going to completely change when the Messiah comes. The sun would still rise and set, people would still have to work for a living. The lion lying down with the lamb was, he taught, a metaphor for former enemies living in peace. Presumably, then, the rules of nature, which have lambs running for cover when lions come around, will still go on. The only difference will be that we will be in a world of peace and justice. But we would have to do so with the natural world existing pretty much as it does now.

Ralph Kramden knew this all along. The world will become Park Avenue but each of us will still have to deal with the furnishings as they are. We will be born, age, become ill, and one day die. There will be joy and sadness in their appropriate times. We'll still have those aches and pains. But the world will feel so different.

We don't bring the Messiah by wishing away the restrictions or disappointments our lives present to us. Instead, we bring the Messiah by working for a world of which we can all be proud, and in which others will find the ways to help us through our problems, and in which we will help others as well.

That brings me to the final thought shared by actor Hugh Beaumont, as Ward Cleaver on *Leave it to Beaver*.

In one episode, his teenage son Wally gripes about his blind date for the dance as she is a few inches taller than he is. This is a veritable crisis in sitcom land and Wally threatens to break their date. Ward decides that the best thing to say to him is that he has to go "and have a good time whether he likes it or not."

Wally reluctantly agrees to the parental suggestion.

Of course he had a good time as his date wears flat shoes but that's not the point.

In the book of Deuteronomy, in a section about the holiday of Sukkot, we read: Vihayita ach sameach, "You will only be happy."

It is of course impossible to mandate happiness but some commentaries point out, you don't have to <u>be</u> happy; you only have to <u>act</u> happy. And, <u>acting</u> happy might lead you to <u>being</u> happy.

So maybe this is the whole point wrapped up into one comment: Act like the Messiah is already here. Don't deny the pains you feel, the disappointments you experience, cry when the time is right. But find one day, one morning, one hour, when you walk outside your home and leave your own concerns behind and say: "I will only be happy. I will act like the Messiah is already here. I will act like our greatest problems are solved."

Don't do it for too long because you might believe it and stop working for the day when it will really come. But at least for a morning or a day, do it and see how it feels. If, by some chance or some divine plan, every person in the world does this at exactly the same time, we will have achieved our greatest responsibility as human beings.

Those, then, are the messages. Open your eyes to everything in this world. Develop a loud, accented conscience. Find your stage and play your part as best you can. Accept that the world will not fundamentally change but that the changes will be in the way we look at life. And, finally, once in a while, act like the Messiah has already come.

We must believe in this myth. We must make it happen. Each of us, each day, must lead this world to the time when we can truly sing: Heenay mah Tov u'mah naeem shevet acheem gam yachad, behold how good and pleasant it is to live together like brothers and sisters, to live our lives in that dream world, that up to now only existed on TV.

My experience of speaking about sitcoms didn't stop there, for when our son Avi was a little boy, I wrote a sermon for the evening of Yom Kippur which was inspired by my ritual of telling him an original story each night at bedtime. Avi loved those stories, which sometimes were take-offs of his favorite TV shows. So I thought of a good bedtime story to share with the congregation based on a TV show. The show was a situation comedy but one you surely would not expect.

A BEDTIME MIDRASH FOR YOM KIPPUR
1995

Tonight I want to tell you something I learned from one of my teachers.

I never sat in his classroom. I never heard him speak. But I have seen him many times. His name was Amos Jones.

You may not recognize his name. But put him together with his friend Andy Brown, connect the two and they become, forever, Amos 'n Andy.

Amos 'n Andy was a popular radio comedy in the'30s and '40s about the lives of two African American men and their families and friends. The widely popular series moved to TV in the '50s.

The show featured some horribly objectionable forms of stereotyping and, as the '50s became the '60s, Amos 'n Andy justifiably became the target of protest. It was appropriately removed from TV in the mid-1960s and has only recently reappeared on video.

Amos 'n Andy experienced a revival because, despite the horrible stereotyping, it was very funny. I still feel guilty laughing because our so-ciety really hasn't changed enough for us to deserve to laugh this way, but it was so very funny and, even more importantly, it had a real, heartfelt touch which was so rare in TV comedies. Watch the episodes carefully and you will see a heart and soul missing from most other shows of that era.

Amos 'n Andy also had another thing going for it: a choir. There was always a choir singing during the opening credits and the choir would often sing in the background during the story itself, providing a quasi-religious atmosphere.

My favorite episode of Amos 'n Andy is the Christmas episode during which the choir helped to create an unforgettable moment.

It is Christmas Eve and Amos's daughter, Arbadella, can't sleep. She's just too excited to close her eyes. So her father sits next to her on her bed and, to the accompaniment of the choir singing in the background, Amos Jones shares a midrash with his daughter. He takes each line of the Lord's Prayer and explains it to her, phrase by phrase, so that she'll understand the true meaning of Christmas and find the peace needed to close her eyes.

He begins: "Our Father which art in Heaven...that means, father of all that is good where no wrong can dwell...Hallowed be thy name...that means that we should love and respect all that is good..." He continues with a beautiful basic lesson in his interpretation of Christian theology and ends with "For Thine is the kingdom and the Power and the Glory, that means that all the world and all that is in it belongs to God. And, as we know it and act as if we know it, that, my darling daughter, is the true meaning of Christmas."

Say what you want about Amos 'n Andy, that scene makes me cry every time I watch it...and I watch it often.

Amos Jones showed us how to properly put children to bed on the holiest night of the year. We should all be sharing a midrash with our kids just like he did.

So, when Yom Kippur rolls around, whether or not our children are so excited that they can't sleep at the prospect of confronting God in repentance, we might say to them something like this:

My dear children, we say the Sh'ma together every night. This night, we're going to do it a bit differently.

Sh'ma Yisrael: Listen O Israel. My darling children, this means that we must always keep our ears open to hear the voices of the world: the voices of nature, the voices of love, the voices of God speaking through the beauty of the universe and the potential of the human being.

While you listen, remember that listening is only one of the senses. Our ancestors thought it was the most important but you must use all of your senses as you seek out God's presence.

You can seek God's presence in so many different ways. Whenever you see something or hear something or smell or taste something which awakens your sense of awe and wonder, you are beginning to walk along the path to finding God. Whenever you act in a way which fulfills your potential, which helps others fulfill theirs, which brings the world closer to perfection, you are proclaiming God's presence.

So, listen for the sounds out there, listen and feel the evidence of God in your lives. Then, do something else when you hear the words Sh'ma Yisrael. Don't only read it as "Listen Israel," read it as well; "Listen to Israel." Listen to the voices of your people. Hear the voices of pain and anguish from those in need whom you are obligated to help. Hear the voices of study and prayer whose example shines for you. Take advantage of every opportunity to hear the voices of the bride and groom under the huppah and celebrate with them. Listen to the cry of the baby at the brit milah and hope for and work for his future as a Jew.

Make these your sounds. Make them your noise. Listen and learn them well so that you can echo them to the next generation, adding your own voice to the choir which has accompanied and encouraged Jewish life for so many generations.

Ado-nai Elohaynu: The Lord our God.

First, my child, you should never forget that God is with you. The Lord is always our God. Of course, you will have doubts as I do. But when you do, seek to experience God's presence. You will find it comforting and nurturing, loving and teaching. These experiences may not happen every day. But when they occur, even when you recognize them only in retrospect, they will change your life.

But, my children, don't ignore the challenge in those two Hebrew words. Ado-nai is singular: My Lord. Elohaynu is plural: Our God.

Never forget that while you should find comfort in the image of God that Jewish tradition has presented you, the concept of your own personal God is even more important. You write your own theology in the final analysis, not teachers, not rabbis, not Jewish tradition. You must decide what you think. You should be willing to join with others and pray to <u>our</u> God, but you must be thinking about <u>your</u> God as well.

While we're on that subject, never forget that "my" and "our" are both essentials in Jewish life. You are only as holy as we are; we are only as holy as you. You are never complete alone. We are never complete without you.

Ado-nai Echad: God is one.

You've learned that since you were two years old. But what does it mean? Yes, it means that there is only one power of creation, not "many gods," only One God.

But it also means that if human beings and the world are created in God's image, the world must be one as well.

Never turn your back on what is happening to others, whoever they are, because your fate is wrapped up in theirs. Never forget that the person down the street or around the corner or across the world is as holy, unique, and infinite in potential as you are. Never forget that God's goal for us is that we make this world one: that we put the pieces together and live in harmony with ourselves, with others, and with the entire world.

Never forget that last part, my children. After all, living in harmony with ourselves, with the world, and with God, brings us to a state of at-one-ment which is what this Day of Atonement is all about.

Let me leave you, my children, with words inspired by my teacher Amos Jones: "If you know this and act as if you know it, that is the true meaning of Yom Kippur."

Go to sleep now and dream of all that your lives and all that the world can be. Then, wake up tomorrow and make it happen.

Sh'ma Yisrael, Ado-nai Elohaynu, Ado-nai Echad.

I know I've spent too much time watching TV over the years. But I've come to believe that wisdom can certainly come from unexpected places, and I've truly learned from all of my teachers, even those I have never met, and even those who lived nowhere else but on television.

Thanks, Nana, for introducing me to Lucy.

Thanks, Nana, also for teaching me that life isn't always easy, that we don't always get the answers we want, and that we might have more difficulties than we think we can face. But sometimes, what we really need is to say to the world: *"too damn bad about you,"* grab ourselves by our own bootstraps and get on with our lives.

4

To The Top of The World –And Beyond

One summer, during my high school years, I immersed myself in a rather odd pastime: I started collecting airline timetables. If you had asked me then, I'm sure I wouldn't have been able to tell you why. But in retrospect, it's obvious. My life was boring.

Those timetables were the closest that I could come to escaping without leaving the comforts and security of home, something I didn't yet have the nerve to do. The countless hours I spent looking at the schedules of flights and devising routes to exotic-sounding places served as a great diversion and also was a glimpse at who I really am, at least in my dreams. At heart, I am an explorer.

You wouldn't know it by looking at my decidedly non-adventurous life as I don't really have the courage necessary to explore on a grand scale. Given the opportunity, though, I love a reasonable adventure.

As I left my teenage years behind, I had more flexibility and greater opportunity to turn my dreams of travel into reality. But other much more important things got in the way. Instead of taking the usual student travel adventures, I spent my summer vacations during rabbinical school and during my first years as a rabbi working at Camp Ramah in New England where I did have the chance to try my hand at canoeing and hiking, but where most of my adventures were of the more cerebral kind.

Then, thank God, I embarked on a different adventure as a father, and began to live vicariously through the experiences of my more daring children, watching them do the things I didn't have the courage to do.

But we can't give up on all of our dreams and I still grab an adventure or two here and there.

The latest evidence of this adventurous spirit is a hobby I have picked up called geocaching. Depending on how you look at it, geocaching is either the perfect diversion or a monumental waste of time. Obviously I think it is the former and even though at first it drove my family crazy, now they love it too, God bless them.

Armed with a GPS which, to borrow a phrase from *Pirke Avot, Ethics of the Fathers*, is supposed to be able to tell you "where you came from and where you are going" and with information from the Geocaching website, a geocacher searches for one of the millions of "geocaches" hidden by similarly obsessed individuals around the globe. A geocache is a container usually filled with trinkets and a logbook where you can sign your name to prove you were there. Sometimes, the boxes don't even contain trinkets, some just have a log. But it doesn't matter what's in the cache. Whatever is or isn't inside, it is the thrill of the search that is important, and I find geocaching an absolutely delightful and engaging way to spend time.

Using my GPS and the longitude and latitude supplied by the website, I've found geocaches around the corner, across the country, and across the world and each time I find one, I feel a sense of accomplishment that I can't quite describe. In that moment, I am Columbus seeing the New World, Archimedes running down the street naked yelling: "Eureka" – an adventure I guarantee you I'll never have.

It's at this point that Ellen would probably say: "You don't get out much, do you?" But at least she says it in a more sympathetic tone of voice and choice of words than my mother used when she told me to "get off your fat ass" because I was spending too much time reading the airline timetables. In a way Ellen's right: life as a rabbi tends to be a bit confining and grabbing a few hours out in the country is sometimes a rare experience. But that's not the only reason I love every minute of the geocaching.

For as long as I can remember, I have loved going to places I've never been to or seeing places I know well from a different angle. One of the reasons that I longed to visit California was to see the sun set instead of rise over the ocean. Closer to home, when I first learned to drive, I would take the car through our neighborhood and turn left where we always turned right and found streets I had never seen, with views I never knew existed. Now, I do that with my geocaching tools, looking for the places around the corner that I have never experienced or off the main roads in cities or towns we pass through.

But there's more to life than geocaching.

We love to travel with the kids and the vacations have been memorable. To expand our itinerary, we had promised them that instead of a fancy Bar or Bat Mitzvah party, we would take a family vacation to a place of their choosing. Avi chose Alaska and we arranged for the exciting cruise/ rail tour complete with shore excursions and all the pampering that comes with it.

As usual, I emulated my Dad and began to prepare for the trip with great interest, buying guidebooks and narratives of life in the "Last Frontier." I even made it through all of James Michener's *Alaska* and found it extraordinarily instructive. But the more I read and planned, the more my father's memory came to mind and I realized it's not the "Dobrusin way" to take a trip by someone else's book.

I knew that the cruise would be great and we lined up some exciting extras, but something was definitely missing. I couldn't bear to think that I was going to do what every other tourist to Alaska did and I feared we would never get off the beaten path.

So, as a surprise to the kids and despite Ellen's uncertainty, I was determined to blow more of our hard earned savings on an extra piece of the trip which I was sure would be unforgettable. I just didn't know what it would be.

I searched the Internet for weeks and finally found something that sounded like what I was looking for: a one-day excursion above the Arctic Circle to the town of Barrow, the northernmost town in the United States. It seemed like it could be a once-in-a-lifetime experience and the explorer in me couldn't pass it up.

I'm so glad that I didn't.

The cruise was great but that last day in Barrow stands out for me as one of the highlights of the entire trip. Even though I tried rock climbing and we went whale watching and white water rafting, Barrow was, for me, the high point of our adventure.

We flew in by plane over the Arctic ice fields and waited at the Barrow Airport for the vintage school bus which would serve as our tour vehicle while the August snow swirled around. When the bus arrived, we began our adventure: dipping our toes in the Arctic Ocean, watching Inupiat Eskimos perform chants and dances, talking to native women selling crafts, listening to our guide tell us about whaling and all of the other elements of the local culture – every moment of the day was fascinating.

I have never forgotten Barrow and I yearn to go back there. I like to say that I want to go to volunteer there in some way – to help the residents of this area who obviously are in need of certain skills from the civilization of the lower 48. Such a selfless thought is admirable. But it isn't the real reason I want to return there. Truthfully, what I really want is to learn from them and to understand more deeply what it feels like to live on the edge of the world. I want to stand on that forlorn but beautiful shoreline one more time. I want to imagine myself as a whaler or an Eskimo guide, hear the stories of their journeys and experience them vicariously.

I have loved all of my journeys: real and imaginary. But as a child of the 1960s, no journey could ever compare with the one I was absolutely convinced I would take one day: I *knew* I would travel to the moon.

I was 14 years old when Neil Armstrong walked on the moon. I remember so many things about that week in July 1969, but my most vivid memory, other than Walter Cronkite's voice booming: "Man on the moon!" was my absolute and unquestioned belief that I would one day walk where Armstrong and Aldrin had walked.

When I was a kid, I never really believed I would own a computer that could fit in my pocket, but it seemed perfectly reasonable to me to assume that if a man could walk on the moon in 1969, I would be able to do so by the time I was 30 or 40.

It took some time for it to sink in that it was never going to happen. I suppose I realized it before the Challenger disaster, but that horrible tragedy ended whatever future I had as a space traveler as it did for so many other millions of Americans. I cried that day for the Challenger astronauts, but I admit that I was also crying for my suddenly less exciting future.

Despite this, I couldn't get rid of the space bug that I had caught so early on. It has been part of me from as early as I can remember. I distinctly remember running outside to see one of the early communication satellites passing overhead. I remember tracking John Glenn's orbital flight on our small globe at home. Thank God for snowstorms! There was no school that day in Boston.

I remember sitting in my elementary school auditorium a few years later while they schlepped out the big TV so that we could watch the first Gemini mission take off. Most of the other kids weren't paying the least bit of attention and I couldn't understand why they weren't interested. I was hooked and have never let go.

I'm sure I'm not alone. There must be many of us who grew up in the '60s who, while driving down a dark road at night, have imagined that the dashboard of the car was an instrument panel and that the long, lonely highway up ahead would lead to the outer reaches of space as we maneuvered their craft to discover new worlds. I'm quite sure there are others who do this – at least I hope there are.

I wish I could say I understood more of the science involved. I don't. In one of my favorite books, *Rocket Boys*, Homer Hickham describes how watching Sputnik pass by ignited in him an interest in the technical aspects of rocketry. It didn't do that for me. The mechanics and science of it all are still beyond me. But it did ignite a further interest in travel and a greater appreciation for the beauty of the heavens and a yearning too for something beyond.

I have tried to figure out star charts and maps but they remain a mystery. I just know what I know: the three stars in a row are Orion's belt, the handle of the dipper points to the North Star, and every so often something happens up in the heavens that makes us all, or should make us all, look up, marvel and say a blessing to God that created all of this.

I've seen a lot in my life. A few years back, when Mars was at its closest point to the earth, I filmed it through the zoom lens of my video camera, thrilled to see that when I zoomed in, I could actually see a ball rather than a point of light. I've seen Saturn and its rings through a telescope. I think I caught a glimpse of the Northern Lights once but I'm not sure of that one.

But I've missed a lot too. A few years ago, Comet Hale-Bopp, the brightest comet in decades was to visit us – Avi and I had planned to see it from a hilltop a few miles from here. But after all, this is Michigan. They saw it from the rooftops of Greenwich Village for goodness sake, but we couldn't see it out here. A fog bank rolled in at the last minute and left many disappointed people, including Avi and me. I had awakened him out of a sound sleep and bundled him into the car only to turn around a few blocks away from the house because we couldn't even see in front of our faces. That week, I wrote a sermon about the hidden miracles in our lives and how they are even more meaningful than the ones we can see. But that beautiful philosophical lesson couldn't cover up my disappointment. I was heartbroken.

Still I keep looking up and I always keep a little card with me with the traditional blessing one says upon seeing an astronomical phenomenon like a meteor: "Blessed be God who works the acts of creation."

I actually did see something once. I was riding down a country road in Pennsylvania one Saturday night when, all of a sudden, I saw a huge fireball cross the sky right in front of me. I knew right away it was a meteorite. And, of course, I responded by yelling out a blessing.

Actually, I didn't say the blessing in exactly the prescribed way. In fact, I said a much shorter blessing: "Oh s**t!".

While I heard reports from one startled eyewitness after another on the radio, I felt more and more guilty for missing my golden opportunity to say the blessing I had rehearsed for so many years. In the end, though, I realized that my exclamation was a blessing. It was a simple statement of wonder at the moment and I have given myself a break. That type of reaction from an otherwise mild mannered puritanical Bostonian certainly is an expression of awe and wonder our rabbis of old would have approved of.

I keep looking up for an opportunity to say this blessing of awe.

And, while I look, I wonder what is really out there…

SEARCHING FOR A PARTNER
ROSH HASHANA 1997

I want to begin this morning with a quotation from a movie.

"You're an interesting species, an interesting mix. You're capable of such beautiful dreams and such horrible nightmares. You feel so lost, so cut off, so alone. Only you're not. See, in all our searching, the only thing we've found that makes the emptiness bearable is each other."

That quotation comes from the movie: "Contact" in which an astronomer, played by Jodie Foster, reaches the culmination of her life's work by interacting with an alien being who shares these words with her.

*The words are meaningful and are critical for all of us. They are, I believe, an expression of the purpose behind the entire endeavor we call religion. Religion seeks to respond to the fact that we **are** all lonely.*

It seems ironic that loneliness would be an issue in such a crowded, fast-paced world. But I am not referring to the loneliness faced by an individual in daily life. Rather I speak of the existential loneliness we often feel as human beings. We look at ourselves as insignificant in the great scheme of things and our lives sometimes appear to have little impact in the universe.

The Psalmist said it best: "When I look at the heavens, what is the human being?" We stare into the heavens on a dark night and feel so small, so insignificant, so very much alone.

But the Psalmist continues: "What is the human being that you take account of him?" The Psalmist teaches us that our loneliness can be addressed by seeking the "you," the one "out there" who cares, the one to whom each of us matters.

I have always been ambivalent about the word "spirituality." I worry that it connotes an attempt to withdraw into a space **within** us rather than reaching out to interact with our world and with whatever is beyond our world. So, I believe that spirituality must focus on something "out there" as a means to focus on what is "in here." We have to look **beyond** ourselves in order to find something more meaningful **in** ourselves. Otherwise, spirituality becomes merely another self-absorbing arrogance among the many in the world.

Thinking of the importance of searching "out there" leads me to consider three movies which are on my list of favorites: E.T., Close Encounters of the Third Kind, and the movie I referred to earlier: Contact.

In addition to the fact that each raises the question of the existence of extraterrestrial life, they each have a spiritual aspect as well. These movies are all connected with the scientific and theological themes that we are not alone: that there is something "out there" which can make our lives more meaningful.

And they each begin with loneliness.

The central characters in each of these movies are lonely: an orphan, a child of a difficult divorce, and a bored frustrated father. Each of them was looking for something to bring some meaning, some completeness to their lives. Each of the characters finds what they are looking for in a connection with something in the heavens beyond themselves: something which, in each case, teaches, challenges, and elevates them.

The idea that we can grow best by interacting with something beyond ourselves is a cornerstone of Jewish theology, and one character in Contact sums it up beautifully. Referring to his life on an orbiting space station, he says: "My little room has one hell of a view." That statement and the Psalmist's assertion: "You have made the lowly human being of dust and ashes just a little less than the divine" are really one and the same statement. They reflect the essence of a Jewish view of spirituality. Despite our smallness, we are just a little lower than the divine.

In fact, according to the midrash, we are all angels.

In the book of Numbers, the recently freed Hebrews panic when they hear the accounts of the 10 scouts sent in to investigate what the land of Canaan is really like. The spies return and claim that they met up with giants in the land. They say: "We felt like grasshoppers in our own eyes and so we looked to them."

A commentary teaches that God says to them: "I understand that you felt like grasshoppers, that happens to everyone now and then. But how dare you assume you looked like grasshoppers to them! Maybe I made you look like angels in their eyes."

God is furious at the people who assume they look like grasshoppers to others because, in fact, we do look like angels in God's eyes. God looks at us and sees the greatness, the grandeur, and the marvelous creative potential of the human being. God looks at us and sees angels, those who can perform godlike acts on earth.

It is unfortunate that this is not usually the attitude that is exhibited when the subject turns to religion in popular culture. Too often, religion is seen as a means to belittle rather than glorify the human being.

Let me share one clear example.

One of the most brilliant programs in television history is The Twilight Zone. In one of its most memorable episodes, "To Serve Man," the earth is suddenly visited by a race of extraterrestrials called "Kanamits" who appear able to solve every problem Earthlings face and to do so with completely altruistic motives.

The leader of the Kanamits is seen carrying around a book written in an unintelligible alphabet. The story turns when he leaves the book behind at the United Nations. The book's title is finally decoded and it reads: "To Serve Man." Knowing this, the last bit of skepticism and fear is removed and many humans decide to accompany the Kanamits on their spaceship back to their planet for further education in the Eden-like setting they describe.

One who agrees to go is Mr. Chambers, a professional cryptographer. At first he was skeptical but the title of the book convinces him to leave his doubts behind. As he is about to board the spaceship, one of his assistants suddenly appears on the scene screaming: "Mr. Chambers, don't get on the ship. To Serve Man...it's a cookbook!"

He is pushed on board and the ship takes off.

This story strikes me as a clear anti-religious polemic. A person comes down with a book written in a foreign language and tells people their salvation lies "out there." Those who buy into it are swallowed up and have their freedom and dignity taken away. This view of religion is based on fear and dread and portrays faith in God as an endeavor which takes away our independence.

But that is not the way we should look at our faith. We need not approach our interactions with the divine solely from the perspective of fear. We are not grasshoppers. We can be angels.

The search for something "out there" is meant not to make our lives seem less significant. On the contrary, the search is meant to give us the courage to be all that we can be, give us the reason to reach for greater heights. The search is intended to give us shoulders of a giant to stand on so that we can see further.

To return to the movies I referred to, it is important to note that in Contact, E.T., and Close Encounters of the Third Kind, the beings beyond us are experienced as supportive, friendly, and encouraging. In each of these movies, the gentle nature of these aliens empowered the searchers to be touched with courage, passion, and creativity and a desire to go back to deepen the relationships in their lives with enhanced determination to make them work. That became possible since the searchers were less lonely than before. After all, they knew someone cared.

There is a memorable scene from the end of Close Encounters in which human scientists, standing in the presence of aliens who are clearly superior to them in intelligence, take a moment to teach a simple musical scale using hand motions. The alien leader, on the second try, mimics the simple hand motions and smiles a knowing, loving, proud, smile.

This is the paradigm. In the presence of immense power and creative ability, there is still something which is needed and appreciated by the one who is clearly superior. Simply put, we can be teachers.

In his appropriately titled book, "Man Is Not Alone," Abraham Joshua Heschel wrote: "There is only one way to define Jewish religion. It is the awareness of God's interest in man, the awareness of a covenant, of a responsibility that lies on Him as well as on us. Our task is to concur with his interest, to carry out His vision of our task. God is in need of man for the attainment of His ends and religion, as Jewish tradition understands it, is a way of serving these ends."

God, while omniscient and omnipotent, has pulled back some of that power in order to allow for our free choice, free will, and a world to be redeemed by human actions.

Our tradition teaches: "As God is righteous and merciful, so must we be righteous and merciful. As God visits the sick, clothes the naked, comforts the bereaved, celebrates with the bride and groom, so must you do all of these things."

God depends on us to do the real divine work on earth.

That is why, as important as study and prayer and theological searching are, no amount of talk, study, or spiritual feeling can possibly replace acts of loving kindness and the deepening of the relationships between ourselves and those we love, and with our fellow human beings in general. Study, prayer, and introspection must be a means to a greater end. In Judaism, the search is meant not primarily to fill ourselves with spiritual feelings, but rather to inspire us to complete the work that our Creator began.

Of course, our understanding of God cannot be only as the One who encourages kindly and sweetly. We must also believe that we disappoint God terribly when we fail, as individuals and as communities, to complete our work. And that is why judgment is so important and why we speak of – metaphorically, I believe – divine punishment. On balance, though, our relationship with God must be based on our grasp of our potential to do great things and not merely on the smallness of our lives in relation to our Creator.

We used to tell a joke when I was growing up. One day, a person died and went to heaven and, on his first walk around with his personal guide, he saw a figure wearing a Boston Red Sox uniform with a big number 9 on the back hitting balls 400 feet into the clouds. The man turns to his guide and said: "Wow, look, it's Ted Williams."

His guide answers him: "Oh, that's not Ted Williams, that's God, he likes to pretend he's Ted Williams."

This joke reveals a fascinating proposition. To put it in irreverent, somewhat blasphemous terms, God's greatest wish, a wish never to be fulfilled, is to be a human being who could experience first-hand the joys and the triumph of being human. Much like a parent who watches her children grow and wishes she could do the things over again, but realizes that she will have to settle for enjoying things vicariously through her children's experience and growth, we human beings by our actions fulfill God's dreams.

Let us continue our search but let us realize that what we are really searching for is more encouragement to do what we know is right all along: making the most of our lives as human beings and thus bringing satisfaction to God and redemption to our world.

I have never seen a UFO, I have never communicated with any extraterrestrials and I assume I never will.

But you never know.

In the meantime, I'll keep looking up, believing with complete faith that there is someone out there looking back from a different angle. Like I did at Barrow, I'll keep looking up from these sometimes beautiful, sometimes forlorn shores, searching for the top of the world...and beyond.

5

The Diamond

I was five years old when we left our summer cottage for the last time. In addition to the walks on the beach, visits to the amusement park, and the hot summer days, there are two memories from those summers that I didn't mention previously.

First, there were my imaginary playmates who lived behind the house in the tall grass. They followed me back home after the summer and stayed around for a year or so after we had left Winthrop behind.

Then, there was the game I used to play when my brother wasn't around. I would take a wiffle ball and throw it up in the air three times. I would swing my big yellow bat, missing each time, and say: "one out, two outs, three outs." Then, after a few innings, I would go inside.

It was always a pitcher's duel.

Yes, I have always been a baseball fan.

I have loved the game from as far back as I can remember. I love the statistics, the smell of the ballpark, the beauty of a game-winning home-run, a classic double play, or an outfielder throwing out a runner at the plate.

But baseball is more than just a game. It is, of course, wrapped up in the heritage and culture of America.

I believe as well that baseball is wrapped up in the culture of Judaism and in Jewish faith. Before I relate more of my personal story and my own passion for the game, here is one of the less personal, more philosophical sermons I gave on the subject.[1]

THE THEOLOGY OF BASEBALL
1991

It is perhaps apocryphal, but it is said that Solomon Schechter, the founder of the Conservative Movement, once told rabbinical students at the Jewish Theological Seminary: "Gentlemen, in order to be a success in the American rabbinate, you must be able to talk baseball."

Baseball, the epitome of American popular culture, was always a language rabbis had to learn. We must have learned it well, for baseball has been a passion of so many Jews throughout the decades.

But the connection of Judaism and baseball goes beyond the fact that it is a ticket into American society. In so many ways, baseball presents the perfect midrash for Judaism.

I base much of my thought on this subject on the writings of one of my heroes, past President of Yale University and Commissioner of Baseball, the late Bart Giamatti. Whenever I read Dr. Giamatti describing baseball, I think that he might very well be talking about Judaism.

I told this to Dr. Giamatti in a letter I wrote to him, and he was truly interested and so very gracious. We exchanged more letters and in a letter responding to my note of congratulations when he was named President of the National League, he added a hand-written sentence at the bottom of the typed letter: "I shall treasure your encouragement. We clearly see things in the same way." I have never felt so honored.

In his book, **Take Time for Paradise**, Giamatti wrote that baseball "is based on the symmetry and order to which all human beings aspire...Our national plot is to be free enough to consent to an order that will enhance and compound – as it constrains – our freedom."

The giving of the Torah immediately after the Exodus from servitude in Egypt shows the enhancing and compounding effect that a willing consent to order can have on our lives. We count the Omer, the days

---

1 Portions of this sermon were originally published in *Moment* Magazine.

between Pesach – the celebration of our freedom – and Shavuot – the commemoration of our receiving the Torah – to express this connection and to celebrate that we are free enough to allow ourselves to be guided by Jewish law and tradition.

But observance of Jewish law is not a simple matter and Dr. Giamatti helps us to understand two of the most elusive terms in Jewish thought regarding religious ritual. He writes about baseball's structure: "Symmetrical demands in a symmetrical setting encourage both passion and precision."

Passion and precision are perfect definitions of two Hebrew words which are so often seen as opposites but which need to co-exist: kavannah and keva. The passion of the inspiration to serve God and bring meaning to our lives (kavannah) is balanced with the objective specifics of Jewish law (keva). The two must live side by side. As Abraham Joshua Heschel taught: "Kavannah is beautiful but has no outlet without the precision the law provides and the keva of the law can not sustain itself without passion."

We need precision to direct the passion and we need passion to continue to find the need for precision.

And that passion and precision has an ultimate goal. Giamatti believed that baseball represents the drive that we all have to leave home and to return, to travel away from our starting point and then to come back to it. He spoke of a runner going the long way around, longing to return home to the place where "one first learned to be separate and [that] remains in the mind as the place where reunion, if it ever were to occur, would happen."

From the perspective of Jewish philosophy and mythology, this is as basic a statement as we can make about our lives. As human beings, we left the Garden of Eden to find our way through the world and bring ourselves and the world we live in back to the Garden, complete and whole again.

But it is not an easy journey. Like the batter rounding the bases, our ancestors took "the long way around." God took us through the desert on a wandering path. This was as a result of our ancestors' sin of disloyalty, but it also had a purpose of its own: that we grow and experience the full measure of life, so that our return would be more meaningful and better appreciated.

Just like the batter rounding the bases, we can only achieve our ultimate goal if we take a long way around, relishing the experiences and recognizing the possibility that even if we do not reach our final destination, we will know that we have tried. So as we seek the redemption of the world, we do not look for simple paths. We engage in the difficult questions. We take the difficult risks and keep our heads up as we round the bases in our quest.

I find it fascinating that the shape of the field reflects that circular aspect of the game and of life. But there is another feature of the baseball field that intrigued Dr. Giamatti, and it intrigues me as well.

The foul lines on the baseball diamond, according to Giamatti, "constrain the sudden eruptions of energy" allowing creativity within certain acceptable limits. This creativity is demonstrated by baseball's continual uniqueness as events that never happened before happen daily within the order and structure of the game and its constants.

As Jews, our ritual tradition started at Mt. Sinai, giving structure to our lives by placing limits. But these limits, like the space between the foul lines radiating from home plate, ever widen. They allow us to constantly find new areas in which to develop ourselves and use our creativity. This creativity lets us respond, with Torah, to things that never happened before in our search to adapt to changing realities. The lines are there to guide us but, unlike the parallel sidelines on the football field, the space between the lines widens to inspire us with new worlds to conquer.

The lines of Torah also serve to unify us as a people. If we find ourselves lost in the world, which can be as empty as the outfield in a ballpark, we can always get our bearings by turning home again, to the point of the convergence of the lines, the point when we stood together at Mt. Sinai.

We are unified as a people not because we behave exactly alike but because we trace the roots of our behavior to the same place and the same moment when we all stood and heard God's voice at Sinai. To regain that unity, we can always turn again, towards home.

As baseball has played itself out over the decades, its sages have taught us so much about our journey through the world. Consider these baseball quotations, three of my favorites, and think about what they teach us about our faith and our people.

I'll start with Ernie Banks, the great Chicago Cubs player and later announcer who greeted beautiful days at Wrigley Field with the call: "Let's Play Two."

That is Judaism's call as well. Let's play two, or three, or, God willing, a thousand. Ritual – repetitive constant ritual – is the hallmark of Judaism. We don't wait for the spirit to move us to say a prayer or perform a ritual action, we do it the other way around. We play two. We repeat our actions over and over, knowing that sometimes the action won't result in much meaning, just as there could be, frankly, a boring baseball game.

Despite the potential for boredom and sameness, one day, when we least suspect it, we'll see a fantastic catch or a come-from-behind victory and we're so glad we stayed around to watch.

Similarly, each day we put on tefillin or keep kosher. Each year, we sit in the Sukkah and dance with the Torah. Often they mean everything to us. Sometimes they seem to be significantly less meaningful. But we keep coming back, we keep playing two, we keep believing in the power of ritual to provide us moments of great meaning.

Next, a quick word from the great philosopher Yogi Berra: "When you come to a fork in the road, take it." We experience our Judaism in a world of opportunities that our ancestors never knew: every type of Judaism one could imagine, in every community, physical and virtual. No one has the excuse that they can't find meaning in Judaism. There is something in it for everyone if one seriously looks for it. So, when that fork in the road presents itself, find the right fork for you, even if it is "the road less traveled." Find your path and take it.

And, finally, Jim Bouton, writing in Ball Four, observed that "you spend your life gripping a baseball and then you find out that it was the other way all along."

What a fantastic thought and what a wonderful lesson in Judaism! Our religious rituals have kept us alive. They have protected us and have enriched our lives. They are holding onto us, rather than the other way around. Without them, we are lost.

As Hebrew essayist Ahad Ha'am wrote: "More than Israel has kept the Shabbat, the Shabbat has kept Israel." The rituals, like the sights and sounds and smells of a ballpark, have a hold on us and won't let go.

Let us hold on to our traditions and continue our path "the long way around." Let us have fun as well while we do it, for while life is not a game, it is meant to be treasured and celebrated. Let us take the field each day with energy and excitement ready to play a full nine innings each and every day.

Yes, I've always been a baseball fan.

But let the truth be told. To be precise, I'm actually not just a baseball fan. I am a Boston Red Sox fan. Usually the two work together, although occasionally they seem to be paradoxical. Either way, I am a passionate Red Sox fan.

If you're born in Boston, it's in your blood.

If you know anything about baseball, and probably even if you don't, you know about "Red Sox Nation." That's what three World Series championships in ten years will do for you.

But I was a fan long before the redemption of 2004 and, as the Passover Haggadah says about our journey which went "the long way around," we should start telling the story with the sad parts and then move to the topic of salvation.

Nothing about baseball is sad when you think about it. Even in the losses, there are enough stories to fill entire books and if the losses don't feel so glorious, you still have the memories of green grass and the smells and sounds of the wonderful game.

But still, there is good baseball and bad baseball and I began to cheer for the Red Sox when they were, quite simply, awful.

That was the era when a Red Sox right fielder tried to make a shoe-string catch and missed. The ball hit the top of his foot and flew into the stands for a homerun.

It was the era in which a Red Sox catcher tried to throw a runner out at second base and hit the pitcher in the back of the head, the ball flying into the Red Sox dugout where, I assume, it hurt one of the players on the bench, probably causing him to end up on the disabled list.

It wasn't the best time to be a Sox fan. But it wasn't all bad: there were plenty of tickets available and for 75 cents you could get a grandstand seat.

Everything changed in 1967, when the Red Sox suddenly began to win and people started not only to listen to the games on radio, but to actually care about who won. It was a year to remember for me. I began to prepare for my Bar Mitzvah and I celebrated my team's first trip to the World Series.

It was also my first year at Boston Latin School, the oldest public school in the country. That's a distinction. But one of the school's most important claims to fame is that it is the closest public school to Fenway Park.

In those days, they played World Series games during the afternoon and the first game started right in the middle of the school day. Our teachers, known for their strictness, especially with students who were in the first year, actually cracked a smile or two when news of a Red Sox run reached our ears. They couldn't ignore it. We could hear the crowd from the classrooms. So, after school, with game one still in the fifth inning, everyone streamed towards Fenway to see if we could get in somehow or at least feel the excitement.

I never made it to Fenway that day, preferring to take a detour with a few friends into the TV department at the giant Sears Roebuck store a couple of blocks from the park. There, we gathered with dozens of other fans eating the free popcorn they were passing out and watching the Red Sox lose 2-1.

The next day was Rosh Hashanah but we still managed to watch the Sox beat the Cardinals 5-0 while we ate matzo balls and brisket.

The Red Sox lost the World Series in seven games that year. At least, though, they had the decency to lose the last game 7-2 and never stood a chance. That spared us the agony of the dramatic losses to come.

In 1975, the Sox won the pennant again and met the Cincinnati Reds in the World Series. I decided to mail in an entry to try to get tickets to a game and, sure enough, I received two tickets to game 6. I should have been thrilled but the tickets presented me with a spiritual dilemma. I had just begun to observe the Sabbath more seriously and game 6 was going to be played on Saturday.

In a decision which can only be considered inspired (or stupid), I sold the tickets to a friend on the condition that he sell them back to me for the same price if the game was postponed.

And, *mirabile dictu*, as they say in Latin, it was.

So I bought the tickets back and went off to game 6 on Tuesday evening, October 22, 1975, with my cousin Dave, to be part of baseball history. We watched what has been called the greatest game in World Series history, ending with Red Sox catcher Carlton Fisk's homerun in the 12th inning.

The next night, friends gathered in my dorm room for game 7 with the champagne on ice. In the fifth inning and with the Red Sox leading, Sox pitcher Bill Lee threw a "blooper pitch" which the Reds' Tony Perez hit halfway to New Hampshire and Joe Morgan hit a pop fly single in the 9th and the Sox lost the series.

Then, there was 1978, and the first day of Rosh Hashanah featured the disastrous loss of the Red Sox to the Yankees in the playoff game. Most baseball fans remember Bucky Dent hitting a three-run homerun that changed the entire course of the game. But I remember another, less recognized part in that game that epitomizes what it meant to be a Red Sox fan during the '70s.

The Red Sox were losing 5-4 in the 9th inning and had a man on first, and Jerry Remy hit a line drive to right field, right at Yankee outfielder Lou Piniella. But any veteran Red Sox fan knows the old line, which is not true anymore since they built a second and third deck behind home plate: "In Boston, the sun rises in the east and sets in the eyes of the right fielder." Piniella, blinded by the sun, threw up his hands in utter fear as he had no idea where the ball was. The ball took one big bounce heading for the right field wall and a game-winning, inside-the-park homerun, but Piniella reached out at the last minute and the ball landed in his glove. He claimed he saw it but I don't believe it. Either way, it doesn't matter. Piniella made the play. The Red Sox lost 5-4.

Apples and honey for a sweet New Year, anyone?

In 1986, the Sox made the playoffs again only to fall behind the Angels 3 games to 1 and were losing in the 5th game 5-2 going into the ninth inning and I had to turn the TV off to go lead Kol Nidre Services to begin Yom Kippur with World Series dreams dashed again.

An hour or so later, I was standing on the bima preparing to give my sermon when I noticed several congregants pointing at me with hand motions of some kind. I checked to make sure my microphone worked, that I had my yarmulke on, that my tie was straight, that my fly was closed, that everything else was in order, but they were still making these wild gestures.

After the sermon, I went over to one of them and asked him what was so important. He showed me his transistor radio and told me the Red Sox had won in extra innings.

It was truly a remarkable comeback, but I had a feeling that we were being toyed with, being set up for a bigger disappointment. My instinct came true two weeks later on Simchat Torah night, when the ball rolled through Bill Buckner's legs and that's all too painful to talk about.

Redemption came in 2004, with an unbelievable comeback from being down to the Yankees three games to none and a World Series sweep of the St. Louis Cardinals.

Like Judaism, baseball is about the passing of traditions from one generation to the next, and I will never forget the feeling when I hugged Avi after the last out of that series. I missed my father, a passionate Red Sox fan himself, more deeply that night than I had since the day he died.

Throughout the World Series that year, I lived out one of my wildest fantasies. A good friend of mine, a sportswriter, was being interviewed on the eve of game 7 of the Sox-Yankees series by a sports radio station in Canada when he happened to mention that he had been talking with me a few minutes before. The hosts of the show were so intrigued by a rabbi who was a baseball fan that they wanted to talk with me.

After I ascertained that I wasn't being set up for some kind of practical joke, I jumped at the chance. So on three occasions, during and after the World Series, I was the "guest baseball analyst" on this radio station. The pulpit is great – but this was an experience to treasure, commenting on the Sox and the Series and Judaism and faith and hope. The hosts of the show told me after our last interview, that if I ever wanted to leave the rabbinate, there might be a job available for me.

I actually thought about it for a few minutes. But I couldn't leave just then. My congregation was depending on me. The crowd at services on the Shabbat after the series was huge and on one of the happiest mornings of my life, I gave this sermon:

A DREAM COME TRUE
OCTOBER 2004

This week marked the high point in a life-long love affair.

This is no recent love affair I'm talking about. I learned as a kid growing up four miles from Fenway Park that I had been born into a faith community shared by everyone in New England. After all, we all spend every summer praying at the same sanctuary.

Sox fans know well the meaning of dor l'dor: "from generation to generation." Parents taught their children to love the Red Sox despite that they know this love would eventually break their hearts. The fatalistic attitude is stubborn. My brother got on a plane from Chicago to Miami on Wednesday wearing a Red Sox hat, a few hours before game 4 and was reminded of this by an old grizzled veteran of many baseball seasons who approached him and told him the Red Sox would choke.

Now we know it need not always be that way. Our conversation with our children about baseball will never be the same.

Almost 12 years ago, we welcomed Avi into the covenant of Israel and I shared some words with him on this bima on the day of his brit milah, his ritual circumcision. I took him in my arms and told him that he was the recipient of a great tradition, one which is mocked by many, misunderstood and ridiculed by others, thought of as archaic and meaningless and which would be the source of sadness and struggle, but that he should hold his head high despite the taunts. Everyone looked at me aghast because they know that is not how I frame Judaism for the congregation or for myself. So I quickly explained that I wasn't talking about Judaism, I was talking about Avi being born a Red Sox fan and showed that under the blanket Avi was in, he was proudly wearing a Red Sox sleeper which my parents had brought from home.

Now, I say to you, Avi, and Mickie as well, God willing your son or daughter will wear the same outfit at his brit milah or her naming ceremony but with one difference. You will be able to say to your child what I could never say to you. You will tell your child that their Grandpa Dobrusin actually saw the Red Sox win a World Series. And, God willing, I'll be there to tell the kid the story of that Wednesday night long ago and, maybe, of more such nights to come.

Speaking of grandfathers, my father lived a wonderful, complete life. He wrote some words to be read at his funeral which said that he had no regrets. But I know that in fact he had two.

The first regret was that he never walked on the soil of the land of Israel. His father had done so. His sons had done so, and his grandson did so a few months after his death, and I kept reminding Avi when we were in Israel a few years ago that we were walking for Papa Dobrusin.

But my dad's deepest regret was that he never saw the Sox win a World Series. As I hugged my family the other night, I said to them: "This one was for Papa Dobrusin."

I know this isn't critically important in the long run. Johnny Damon's leadoff homerun didn't bring world peace. Derek Lowe's superb pitching performance wasn't like finding a cure for AIDS or cancer. Manny Ramirez makes more money playing one game than many hard working, honest, good people make in a year, and I know that some of you here today have more on your mind than baseball. But life is to be enjoyed as well, and I'm sure enjoying this.

Being a Red Sox fan has always been about hope and about finding things to believe in, and dreams, both serious and not so serious, to pursue and to hope to achieve. May we never, ever stop believing that the things we wish for – for ourselves, for our children – will come true. They will one day.

Let me close with a reference to a song. I played this song, **Gone at Last** by Paul Simon so often and so loud in the car on Wednesday and Thursday that you've probably heard it already if you were driving anywhere around Ann Arbor.

I've had a long streak of bad luck
But I pray it's gone at last.

May we see the day, as individuals and together as a community, and as a world, in which all our real troubles are gone at last. Until then, may we all pass along to our children the hope that that day will come. This past week, for Red Sox nation, the night we prayed and hoped and wished for really came.

May it come for all of us in our serious struggles bimhayra biyamaynu, speedily in our days.

Yes, the journey is long.

May we all always treasure our path around the bases and may we all see our dreams, big and small, come true.

6

Music and Midrash

Many people talk about how their homes were filled with music when they were kids. I certainly wouldn't go that far in describing our house, but music definitely had its place. My father played the piano by ear, and I can still hear his distinctive style every time I sit down to play. My grandmother used to love to watch Lawrence Welk and although I only occasionally heard her sing, she could tap her foot with the best of them.

Then there was Mom who would try to sing every once in a while often with disastrous results.

Although we had a record player, it was not used very often. But my earliest musical memory is of one scratchy record: Jamaica Farewell by Harry Belafonte. I can't say for sure whether I heard it 10 times or 100 times, but I distinctly remember sitting with Mom listening to the record and wondering for years who the "little girl" was that was left all alone in Kingston-town. I couldn't understand how that man who sounded so nice had left a child all by herself. It bothered me for years. Such is the power music has in our lives.

I have loved music ever since I was a little kid and anyone who ever has driven next to me on the highway while I was in my car alone would recognize that one of my secret aspirations is to be a musical performer. I tend to go through phases in which I listen to one type of music or one performer over and over again and after enough time, like most, I find myself imitating and singing along. So, a few years ago, while I was heading to officiate at a funeral during my *Queen* phase, I sang a great duet with Freddy Mercury on *Somebody to Love*. I still can see the look on the faces of the people in the car next to mine as they caught me, dressed in a grey overcoat and a dark hat giving that great song all of my energy and passion. It must have been quite a sight.

Despite some great performances in the car and in the shower, a career as a musician was not in the cards. My mother vetoed the idea of my taking a part in a local theatre production when I was about 8. My piano teacher had recommended that I audition for a small role but my mother thought it would interfere with school so she said no. I don't hold it against her. I have found my stage in life and I think I am better suited for the *bima* than the concert hall.

My parents did support my music lessons when I was a kid, and my elementary school piano teacher often told me that I could be a very good pianist if only I would practice and learn to play what was on the page before I improvised. I never really learned.

Of course, I knew the truth even at a young age: music is meant to be interpreted. We must read the notes as they are written but we can improvise as well. That is also how we should teach Torah. When giving a sermon, a rabbi will often take a text whose words are set in stone and, adding his or her own personal perspective, aiming to affect the way people will hear the words, in the same way that a musician will interpret a score in his or her own way or a singer who "covers" a song someone else has recorded changes the way the lyrics sound.

A few years ago, when I entered quite unexpectedly into my *Jimmy Buffett* phase, I discovered that he had also recorded *Jamaica Farewell*. I was struck immediately by the power music has to be transformed as it passes from one performer to another. I was caught between the tender memories of my childhood moments with my mother and the challenge of hearing that old familiar song in an entirely different way.

In the live recording I have of Jimmy Buffett playing that song, he introduces it by saying: *"This is for Harry Belafonte. I hope you like what we've done to your song."* That was nice of him to say but whether Belafonte liked it or not, it really didn't matter. Jimmy Buffett's version is out there for all to hear and to choose or reject, as they wish.

When a rabbi uses the text of Torah as a score and orchestrates that text to move people spiritually, he or she knows that some will agree with the interpretation and some will not. That is the beauty of Judaism and of textual interpretation. If you don't like one interpretation, you turn the page and find another.

While nothing takes the place of our holy texts, any text can become a kind of Torah and, for me, there are no more accessible and no deeper texts than those of contemporary music. (Those of you of my age will, I am sure, understand when I say that "contemporary music" to me is anything written or performed from 1960 to 1980.)

I learned about the connection of music to midrash from two individuals. One, of course, was my dad.

My father loved to sing. The songs that he wrote brought him great satisfaction, and he also loved to sing songs other people had written. But when Manny Dobrusin sang a song, he put his own stamp on it, sometimes to the point of doing what we rarely do with holy texts. He didn't only interpret; he changed the words to fit his mood.

Instead of singing "Fly me to the Moon," Dad's subtle adaptation was: "Fly me up a tree." Then, there was one of his favorite serious songs: "I Believe," whose corny but inspiring lyrics: became, on certain days in certain moods: "I believe for every drop of rain that falls...someone gets wet." – followed by a deep laugh.

But there was another inspiration that enhanced my understanding of the connection of music and midrash, a genius for whose work I have the utmost admiration and, truly, awe. If the first song I remember hearing was Jamaica Farewell, the first song I remember learning by heart began with these unforgettable four words: "Hello Muddah, Hello Faddah" and one day I paid tribute from the pulpit to my first musical hero, Allan Sherman, and explained, in great detail what it means to write midrash:

A TRIBUTE TO A TRUE GENIUS
2006

Several people have asked me over the last few weeks: "What's the deal with Allan Sherman?" Hearing that I was going to teach a class in honor of this genius, a lot of folks just shook their heads.

Your cynicism truly shocks me.

Before I continue, let me explain to the uninitiated who this genius was. Allan Sherman was a TV writer and producer who worked with some of the most intelligent comics of the 20th century. During the late 1950s, Sherman developed his own shtick, writing comedic words to old songs or classical pieces of music and became an overnight sensation.

His work is worth remembering for three reasons. First, and most importantly, even after almost 50 years, Allan Sherman's material is what it always was – very, very funny.

Secondly, his songs are period pieces. They remind us what life in general, and Jewish life in particular, was like in America in the mid '60s.

But there is one other reason why I have become enthralled with Allan Sherman's work: his songs serve to illustrate a crucial point about Judaism. And if you haven't been able to understand it no matter how many times rabbis have tried to explain it to you, it is because you haven't thought about it by learning from Allan Sherman. Now, thanks to him, you will understand.

Allan Sherman wrote midrash.

Allan Sherman had a gift. While the rest of the world would hear lyrics and accept them as they were, Allan Sherman would hear something different. The rest of the world was hearing: "Alouette, gentille Allouette" and he was hearing: "Al 'n Yetta always sit together" and turned it into a tribute to 1960s television shows.

The rest of the world heard: "Won't you come home, Bill Bailey?" Allan Sherman heard: "Won't you come home, Disraeli, won't you come home, Come home to Queen Victoria," and turned it into a satire of British royalty.

Finally, while the rest of the serious world was proudly singing "Glory, Glory, Halleluyah," he turned it into "Glory, Glory, Harry Lewis," who worked in Irving Roth's fabric factory and was last seen "trampling through the warehouse where the drapes of Roth are stored."

It is because of Allan Sherman that you rarely hear a serious orchestra play a beautiful piece called Dance of the Hours, by the 19th century composer Ponchielli. This is because the minute the orchestra reaches a lovely, familiar section in the middle of the piece, the audience would most likely start laughing and singing "Hello Muddah, Hello Fuddah." Poor Ponchielli. Then again, maybe it's not so bad. At least his music is still being played.

That is exactly the point. No matter how we twist the p'shat, the intended meaning of the Jewish text we interpret, we are insuring that the source text will continue to be heard and seriously considered. And that is what really matters.

It is not only contemporary rabbis who treat text this way. This is the way we have reacted to text throughout our history.

There is a well-known rabbinic commentary surrounding a verse in Isaiah. The commentary is so beloved that it actually can be found in the daily prayer book.

Isaiah had said: **Kol Banayich**: All of your children should learn of the Lord. But others said: "**Al Tikra Banayich elah Bonayich**" "Don't read it as "your children" but as "your wise ones" or, others say, "your builders," two phrases which sound very similar in Hebrew.

The instructions are clear: "Don't read it this way, read it that way." The text in Isaiah is what it is and can't be changed. But we can change the way we hear it, the way we read it, the way we teach it.

This is the secret of giving a d'rasha, a Jewish interpretation of Torah. When someone gives a d'rasha, she is trying to alter the way you hear the words of the text. She is planting in your mind an interpretation which she hopes will take root and forever color the way you hear those words.

Our responsibility as Jews is to hear something different when a text is read, to have the words make connections for us. We attune our ears to hearing something different than what the words are saying: to hear them with our own ears, to adapt them to our own philosophy, to shape them into a point which we will then share with others.

This is the challenge of hearing Jewish text.

Did Allan Sherman think about this? I'm not sure. But I would assume he went to Hebrew school. In his brilliant version of "On the Street Where You Live," he rhapsodized: "Children learning the Torah, Oh the temples that thrive." Maybe he learned his lesson well and set a paradigm for us.

If that's the case, the way he did it was very instructive as well. He had the wisdom to have the music playing in the background. In fact, he made it a point to get excellent musicians to play very well and we sit back, listen to these great musicians play classical or jazz or folk or pop with all of the musical skill while his words take us to completely different places.

This is the secret of reading and hearing Torah. The music of the original text is playing in the background and we place on top of it the continuing experience of textual interpretation which defines who we are as a reading, listening, questioning people. The music continues and we add our own words, and each of our words is as legitimate as any other because they are said against the background of this beautiful music.

Allan Sherman took his work very seriously. That was his personality and you can hear it in his words. It wasn't silliness. It was a craft which he honed over the years, just like those who study Torah sharpen their own listening and reading skills to the point where they feel comfortable sharing their ideas with others.

This is what it means to read as a Jew. We don't aspire to hear the words of Torah the way someone else did or the way we heard them yesterday. Our hope is to find a chiddush, a new way of hearing the old words. That is what keeps our faith alive.

I have never been able to write music or to write new lyrics to old songs (my brother seems to have picked up that skill from my Dad). But I have always been able to hear holiness in the words of my favorite song writers and find, without changing their words, that a song can be made to either mean something else entirely or perfectly illustrate a point it was not written to illustrate.

So, I frequently find myself on the pulpit quoting the songs that have formed the background music of my life. If my father found great peace in singing the songs he wrote in his last days, I find my voice in interpreting the works of some of my favorites.

The first songwriter I quoted in a sermon in Ann Arbor was my favorite songwriter Harry Chapin. He has always been the one I keep returning to after my obsessive phase with another performer has burned out. A songwriter, storyteller, and social activist, Chapin's work inspires me like none other, and one Rosh Hashanah, I based the conclusion of my sermon on his words.

The sermon was about the importance Jewish tradition places on the experience of dreaming, both literally and figuratively. I found great meaning in the words Chapin wrote to end a song called: "I Miss America" in which he lamented the lack of vision in our nation. He closed with these words:

Well, my little boy he told me something just the other night.
He whispered it as I kissed him before I turned out the light,
And of course he said it simple as only children can
He said: "Daddy, Daddy, Daddy please
I'm ready to dream again"

I related the words to one of the most important of all High Holy Day prayers: Avinu Malkaynu. In this prayer, we address God as "Our Father, Our King." We ask God to forgive our sins and give us another chance even though we don't have the actions that would justify the granting of our petitions.

I ended that sermon in this way:

"O God, we don't have the actions but we do have the dreams. We know what we want and we know what we need and we know what this world could be if we could only act on our dreams."

But of course, to say that sincerely, we really do need to have dreams. We can't ask God to consider our dreams unless we truly take the time to envision a better future, and for that we need to add an additional phrase to Avinu Malkaynu.

The prayer ends: "Our Father, our King, have mercy on us and answer us even though we don't have the acts which should merit our redemption"

If we want to truly appeal to God, we should expand that line: "Our Father, our King, we may not have the acts that argue for our salvation. But this time, God, don't look at our actions but look at our dreams. Look not at what we are but at what we dream of being, look not at the world as it is but the world we dream of.

"Avinu Malkaynu, Our Father, our King," "Daddy, we're ready to dream again."

It was only my second High Holy Day sermon in Ann Arbor and I'm not sure how calling God: "Daddy" went over. But it set me on a course that I continue to follow, and Harry Chapin's words were never far from me or far from my understanding of Judaism.

Chapin wrote about his love for his wife in a song called: "You are the Only Song" which included a phrase: "**And, now when they turn out the spotlights, I'm never sure where I'm supposed to go.**" To me, the singer was Noah, who, after the flood, found no meaning for his life and ended up living out his days in lonely despair. Chapin's line was a warning to all of us to find ways to move on after we have spent some time in the spotlight and had to then share it with others.

Another Chapin song called "Stranger with the Melodies" tells the story of a husband and wife singing team who broke up. The split left the man singing chord patterns over and over again since his wife, the lyricist, was no longer with him.

The song strikes me as a great metaphor for Tisha B'av, the day we consider the distance between ourselves and God and search to recapture the magic of our mutually beneficial relationship in which words and music are intertwined.

Finally, Harry Chapin's beautiful ballad: "Mail Order Annie" in which he tells the story of a pioneer farmer in North Dakota who has ordered a wife from the big city and tries to calm her fears of loneliness with the words: **"But there's you babe and there's me and there's God"** has always been a great opening for teaching about Jewish marriage and the protection and sanctuary the Jewish home provides against the dangers and emptiness of the world.

There are so many other songs by so many other artists that I have found meaningful and that relate naturally to Jewish rituals.

Think of the words of Loggins and Messina in *Watching the River Run*:

"And we go on and on watching the river run, further and further from things that we've done, leaving them one by one..."

This is the perfect song for Tashlich, the Rosh Hashanah ceremony of repentance that takes place on the banks of a river. During Tashlich, we watch the river run, watching the passage of time and realizing that we are one year closer to the mouth of the river with one year of less time to separate us from that which we need to abandon in order to live a full and complete life.

Then there is The Old Songs by David Pomeranz, which talks about a man trying to rekindle a love affair by lighting candles, pouring wine, and playing the "old songs."

What else could he be talking about than Shabbat? The holy time when, with candles and wine, we break out the old songs to bridge the gap between ourselves and God that has grown over the week and over the years. Shabbat is "a glimpse of the time of the Messiah," and maybe the old songs we sing each Shabbat will bring that day of closeness with the divine for all.

Finally, there is one of my favorite "old songs." It was written by Irving Berlin and I first heard it when Ricky Ricardo sang it to Lucy:

Heaven, I'm in heaven
And my heart beats so that I can hardly speak
And I seem to find the happiness I seek
When we're out together dancing cheek to cheek

I know this is a song of romance and, sure, I can be romantic (even though I'm a lousy dancer) but as Yom Kippur approaches, I find that song reflecting exactly what we're supposed to be doing, allowing God to wrap us up into a Divine dance in which our moves fit together and in which we can find a time of unity: "at-one-ment," Atonement.

Of course, it doesn't stop here and I pray it will never stop. For each time the cycle of the year goes around, the songs echo in my mind and I find myself unable to escape the power of the words.

I don't know whether my path to the rabbinate, to marriage, and to fatherhood has been any more of a "long and winding road" than anyone else's. Maybe it's been much more direct and clear than I ever could admit. But I know that, without the background music of my life, it wouldn't have been nearly as meaningful, and without the inspiration of all of these musicians and so many others, I wouldn't have been able to find the words to teach what I most want to say.

As Harry Chapin wrote in Stranger with the Melodies: "**A song don't have much meaning if it don't have nothing to say.**" Music is great. But it's what we hear in the words that changes our lives, and the job of a rabbi is to help people hear different meanings in the lyrics which are always around us.

I demonstrated that one Yom Kippur in my sermon before the Yizkor Service. I assume few of my congregants expected to hear the lyrics of a song like the one I referred to from the bima. But I saw many mouthing the words as I quoted one of my favorite songs with a definite purpose in mind.

TWO OUT OF THREE
YOM KIPPUR 2008

I decided on the subject that I wanted to address during this sermon two months ago. I wrote a first draft and I liked it but I knew it needed something. It needed a twist to make it interesting and memorable and I couldn't come up with it.

So, I did what I often do when I am faced with a situation like this – I got in my car and took a drive in the country.

It was a lovely day but the drive wasn't helping. I still could not think of the missing piece. After a while, I became frustrated and started to turn back for home. As I did, I noticed there was a CD loaded in the car's CD player. Without knowing what it was or which member of my family had put it in, I decided to turn it on.

Let me assure you that I do not believe that God sends messages through CD players. But maybe I should consider it because the song that came on provided the perfect missing piece to the sermon.

I don't believe the song was meant to be a theological statement, but others by the same writer have a strong spiritual element to them so I'm not prepared to completely dismiss that possibility. Either way, though, I am not being irreverent when I suggest that there is some wisdom in this song, whose most popular version was recorded by a singer, with the decidedly inappropriate (for Yom Kippur) name of Meat Loaf, to help us understand a very serious spiritual issue.

The song is called: Two out of Three Ain't Bad.

Some of you will recognize the song and some won't. But it really won't matter in the long run because my sermon today is not about the song but rather about a book.

The book, written 30 years ago by my colleague and teacher, Rabbi Harold Kushner, is called When Bad Things Happen to Good People.

Rabbi Kushner's son, Aaron, was a victim of a terrible disease called Progeria, otherwise known as Rapid Aging Syndrome. Aaron died at the age of 14 in the body of an old man. Throughout Aaron's illness and after his death, Rabbi Kushner faced a theological crisis as all of the lines he had heard as a student and all of the lines that he had said in his role as a rabbi suddenly sounded hollow in this changed reality that he faced. How could a rabbi continue to preach, how could a Jew continue to pray, how could a person continue to believe having faced this reality?

Rabbi Kushner decided not to hide from the issue but to think it through. After much contemplation and after reading through Job and other sources of wisdom, he had a startling realization. He took out his pen, because that's what we did 30 years ago, and wrote out three simple statements which he said all people who believe in God would like to believe:

1) God is all-powerful and directly causes everything that happens in this world.
2) God is just and fair and stands for people getting what they deserve in this world so that the good prosper and the wicked are punished.
3) Job -- or Aaron Kushner -- was a good person.

Rabbi Kushner writes: "As long as Job is healthy and wealthy, we can believe all three of these statements with no difficulty. When Job suffers, we have a problem."

And, whenever one has experienced deep sadness or has felt the pain of someone else in the world which can be so cruel, that problem surfaces again.

Knowing he could never give up believing in God, Rabbi Kushner felt he had to eliminate one of these three statements in order to continue to believe. He would not abandon his belief that his son was basically a good person and he concluded that to believe in an unjust God, one who did not stand for fairness and justice, was senseless and offensive.

That left only one of the three sentences to eliminate. So he came to the conclusion that to believe in an all powerful God who is involved in every act that takes place in the world and in every aspect of our lives and treats us based upon our adherence to commandments or to ethical living is indefensible, untenable, and potentially hurtful as well.

Rabbi Kushner looked at those three sentences about God's omnipotence, God's goodness and his son's innocence and concluded (and these are my words) that "Two out of Three Ain't Bad." He decided that he would rather believe in a God who was not all-powerful than to give up his faith in God's goodness or Aaron's.

Kushner wrote his book so that people who felt distant from God, feeling that God's touch was so cold that they, like the singer of the song, were in fact "crying icicles instead of tears," could find comfort in believing in God again. They could believe although the expectations were different. They could believe in God who was not giving them protection from pain but sympathy, comfort, and encouragement when the world turned against them.

Rabbi Kushner teaches this approach with hesitation. He admits that something is lost when you give up this belief in an omnipotent God. He writes: "In a way, it was comforting to believe in an all-wise, all-powerful God who guaranteed fair treatment and happy endings, who reassured us that everything happened for a reason, even as life was easier for us when we could believe that our parents were wise enough to know what to do and comforting enough to make everything turn out right. But... it worked only as long as we did not take the problems of the innocent seriously. When we have met Job, when we have been Job, we cannot believe in that sort of God any longer."

I believe he is right. I believe his theology makes perfect sense and it has guided my thought and my interactions in my own life and in my rabbinic work.

But the story can't stop here because thirty years later, there is a question that has to be asked: Is it good for the Jews?

By that I mean two things. First, can we sustain a belief in God and build a traditional Jewish life of prayer and ritual around a belief in a God who does not directly impact our daily lives? Is this blunt honesty or is it the first step towards denying the existence of God altogether and undermining everything our teachers have taught for millennia?

Secondly, does it really help people? Is it fair to leave people with this answer or is it ultimately unsatisfying?

Let me address the second question first.

No matter how clearly or passionately I or anyone else might present this idea of limited divine power, it does leave us with some serious issues. There are those who reject it entirely, preferring to ignore the question or to embrace the more traditional answers: "We can't understand God's actions." Or, "Everything will be explained to us in the world to come." Or, God forbid, "We should have fasted on Yom Kippur (or checked our mezuzahs more often)."

I understand the reason people choose to believe that God punishes those who aren't loyal to the covenant or aren't the best people they can be. Such beliefs underscore the importance of being good. They underscore the importance of observing the traditions. But the pain and the guilt that this belief can cause is so deep and so damaging. To even suggest that directly or indirectly God punishes with devastating illness those who do not keep kosher is a hillul hashem, a desecration of God's name.

Still, some see Kushner's approach as an unreasonable alternative and too great a challenge. They think it is wrong to expect that people in the midst of terrible agony can accept a complex idea and would want to struggle with a thorny and somewhat paradoxical theological concept. For some, it is better to accept a clear statement defending God or claiming we can never know God's reasons or denying that God exists. For some, the comfort lies in having a definitive answer while Kushner's answer may be seen as weak and defensive.

Then, there are those who have accused him and others who hold this opinion as engaging in "theological gerrymandering" -- trying to structure God's role in the world so that it includes just what we want and excludes everything else. I accept that criticism but would argue that a theology that causes us pain or runs counter to what we see in the world with the hope that it would make us better people doesn't work for everyone. In addition, it is important to note that, for Rabbi Kushner, the idea of this theology is not to take responsibility away from us but to envision God as teacher and to help us to become God's agents and God's angels on earth bringing comfort, support, and love to those who so desperately need it.

This theology works for me. It is honest, constructive, and thoughtfully sensitive. It leaves me with far fewer unanswered questions than any of the other approaches that I have ever heard. But theology is personal and one size does not fit all.

Then, there is the other issue. If God can't or, as I prefer to think of it, has willingly stopped interacting in history at one point after the Exodus and Sinai, then why in God's name would we waste time praying: why would we say a Mishebayrach blessing asking for God's healing? Why would we pray for rain when there is a drought? Why would we pray for God to protect our family or our people?

If God can't control any of these things, why bother to pray at all?

What do we need God for if God can't do what we need God to do?

For these questions, I have answers.

We do need prayer. We need prayer to remind ourselves and remind God what is important to us whether or not we can expect a tangible response. We need prayer to bind us together in a community reaching for something greater. We need public prayer to remind others how much we need the community's help in supporting us as we face difficult times. We need the comfort of community and the comfort of believing we are not alone.

We do need God in our lives. We need hope and we need faith: faith in God, faith that living correctly makes our lives and our world better in the long run, even if some days bring disappointment or even tragedy. We need faith to believe that this story that we are all writing together will someday have a happy ending in a redeemed world.

We even need faith in answered prayers and in miracles which, when they occur, seem to contradict Rabbi Kushner's belief in God's limitations.

Yes, it seems prayers are sometimes answered and divine miracles occasionally do occur, and I celebrate them joyfully and praise God even at the risk of being inconsistent in my theology. But some prayers are not answered and miracles don't happen to everyone and they don't happen every time, and I refuse to believe that God plans miracles only for those who perform the right rituals or who say the right words or who are in some sense deserving. The Talmud tells us: Ayn Somchim al Hanays, "We do not depend upon miracles" and we don't question our merit or blame ourselves if the miracle doesn't happen for us or someone we love.

But even when the prayer is not answered or the miracle doesn't occur, we must continue to believe that God cares. We just need to know where to look for proof. The Torah says that when Moses asked God if he could see the Divine face, God said: "You can only see My back." A traditional commentary explains: "You may not see Me clearly but look back on a situation and you will see where I have been," in the face of a friend who cared, in a doctor who tirelessly worked to bring healing, in the sense of comfort brought by a familiar song or word of prayer. That is evidence of God's caring and that comfort is real.

When I see you, God forbid, in times of horrible tragedy, I remember what Rabbi Kushner taught us at the Seminary one day. He taught us that Job's friends only got in trouble when they started to talk. Sometimes the best I can do is to offer my presence. Sometimes, silence is the best answer.

But you still have a right to ask: Why? Why did this happen to me?

And, because I have no other answer to give and because even at times of pain I need to be honest, I will say to you: "I don't know why. But as the psalmist says: 'I am with him in your trouble.' I believe with perfect faith that God is crying with you now. It is precisely at times of tragedy that people need God the most, to believe in a God who can't change the past or even the future but who is there to support us, to cry with us, to encourage and inspire us and, yes, even to be the object of our anger."

Our tradition has always encouraged and modeled screaming out in anger against God and I believe that it is perfectly reasonable and acceptable to scream out against God in the face of tragedy. But I would humbly suggest that if you are going to blame God, you should blame God specifically for creating a world in which free will and natural consequences rule. Don't blame God for singling you out to receive such pain because that can't be the way God works.

Blaming God for the world that God created rather than for bringing pain to your life does make a difference. As the world goes on and as we, God willing, recover at least somewhat from the tragedy that we have faced, we might come to accept the fact that a world of free will and natural consequences is much better than a world in which we are merely puppets being orchestrated by God. Occasionally, when life is so bad to us, we might like that comfort, but being a free human being is, on balance, far better.

I know that there are still unresolved theological questions. I don't and I can't speak for God. But I believe that no one is singled out for tragedy in this world. I believe that God cries with us and I believe that we need God in our lives even if all of the serious theological gymnastics don't satisfy us.

The Torah commands us to love God and despite what we will hear later this morning when we read about the martyrdom of Rabbi Akiva who said he loved God even as his life was taken in such a cruel way, for most of us, loving God at times of great sadness is impossible. No one should apologize for finding it difficult or impossible to love God when in the midst of suffering.

So, let me return to Meat Loaf and my song for the day. As many of you no doubt know, his "two out of three" were:

"I want you, I need you but there ain't no way I'm ever going to love you."

I believe God says something very similar: "I want you to want me and to need me even if you can't love me at this moment." Two out of three, dayenu, that is enough for now.

But now isn't forever and nothing in life is set in stone, and that's why we should never say to God: "There ain't no way I'm **ever** going to love you" because no matter how dark and cold the world may appear now, one day the sun may shine brightly enough or at just the right angle to melt away the icicles and bring you not only to want God and to need God but to love God and God's world again.

May we all be blessed with comfort and with the peace of God's embracing presence. No matter what each of us believes about God, may we never forget that we are God's agents of comfort in the world God created.

The writer of "*Two out of Three Ain't Bad*," Jim Steinman, sums up this entire subject for me.:

> **If you hold onto a chorus, it can get you through the night...**
> **There's always something magic.**
> **There's always something new.**
> **And when you really, really need it the most**
> **That's when rock and roll dreams come through**

He was speaking about the power of music but what he says about Rock and Roll is true about Torah as well for me as for so many. There is always something magic and new when we listen seriously to the words of the Torah and they tell us to do exactly what the songwriter claimed Rock and Roll does: help us to "keep on believing."

Torah helps us always to "keep on believing," especially when we sing it in a way which reflects the melody and lyrics of our lives.

7

Love

Ellen and I were formally introduced to each other at a dinner in the home of mutual friends. During the meal, the neighbor's dog decided to wander into the house and take up a space under the table. The attention that we both paid to the big black lab helped bridge some of the awkwardness of our first meeting. If, as our tradition teaches, God actually spends time making "shidduchs" – bringing couples together – then clearly this dog was an angel in the truest Jewish sense of the word.

We share a love of dogs and animals in general and, shortly after that first dinner, I was introduced to Silky, Ellen's chocolate lab mix, who two years later would officially become my "stepdog."

Silky was one of the most remarkable creatures I have ever met. She was smart. In fact, she was almost too smart as we actually had to spell things that we didn't want her to understand. She had a heart of gold and, after a few hesitant days during which she acted like a chaperone, Silky decided to defend and protect me as she had done for Ellen. When the kids came, she accepted them and loved them without question. One of my favorite photos is a picture of two-year-old Mickie sitting on the couch watching TV with Silky sleeping soundly with her head in her lap.

Silky loved to take walks and it was during my first days of walking her that I realized how great an audience a dog can be. She would listen to my sermons and my ideas for classes and always approved. I began to find that I developed some of my best ideas on those walks.

In many ways, Silky and I grew older together and in March 2001, when I came home after sitting shiva in Boston for my father, she came right up to me as I walked in the door, put her head down and cried. She did not leave my side for hours.

When it came time, a few months later, for us to say good-bye to her, I cried like I had never cried before.

We decided that we would wait until spring to think about bringing another dog into our home. But our plans changed abruptly that fall.

Everyone, of course, was shocked and stunned by the events of September 11, 2001 and those who lost loved ones bore the greatest and heaviest burdens. However, rabbis had a particularly unique if considerably less serious challenge to face in that September 11 occurred one week before Rosh Hashanah and we all had to throw away our carefully planned sermons and take time from the mourning and grieving to write something meaningful for that day. On the day after Rosh Hashanah, September 20, I was absolutely drained with no energy to think, no desire to go to my office, and none of the necessary concentration to finish my planning for Yom Kippur. I called Ellen at work in a panic.

She made a great suggestion: "You need to get out of the office and go to the Humane Society and walk a dog." I realized how right she was. I had so much missed my beloved friend Silky with her ears which were such a comfort to scratch. So I said: "Good idea" and hung up just as Ellen was saying: "But don't fall in love."

It was too late.

I walked into the Humane Society and asked if I could walk a dog and they said: "We just got one in that needs a walk." And out came Buddy, a four-year-old yellow lab. He took one look at me and ran to get his suitcase.

That afternoon, the entire family came up to meet him and he charmed them all. But we had to wait a week in case someone claimed him.

We renamed him Benny and each afternoon I brought Benny a dog biscuit and took him for a walk around the grounds of the shelter. I even told him my sermon idea for Yom Kippur and he clearly approved. We were bonding so wonderfully and I started filling out the papers to take him home. They told me he would be ours on Thursday the 27th which was, of course, Yom Kippur.

So I casually mentioned that I couldn't get him until the next day and they casually mentioned to me that if I didn't, they would give him to someone else as there was a waiting list. I was distraught, even to the point of trying to find some justification in Jewish law for me to drive up to the Humane Society during the break in the services and pick him up. The standoff continued for a few minutes until another employee put an end to this foolishness by threatening to call the local newspaper with the story if they didn't let me have him.

Thankfully it all worked out and Benny came home the day after Yom Kippur – not to take Silky's place, of course, but to be a different kind of loyal friend. He brought joy, love, and a quiet dignity into our home until the day he died.

We like to say that when they were handing out sweetness and love, Benny was at the front of the line but couldn't find his way to the "brains" line until it was too late. Of course, that's unfair; but whatever he lacked in vocabulary recognition, Benny more than made up for in his temperament and his class.

Benny served as a therapy dog at a local hospice and could charm his way through every human interaction he was exposed to. He was loyal without question, completely undemanding and such a wonderful part of our family.

One way in which his loyalty came through most clearly was with his total acceptance of the other four-legged members of our family. Mickie so dearly wanted a kitten and the four cats we have had in our home: Lewy, Jimmy, Spot, and Ozzie, all rescue cats, each in his time have been a delight. They became part of our home and Benny didn't bat an eyelash.

Having cats in the house has been a rather significant revelation for me. While I do love all animals, I had never really understood the attraction of cats but these guys (maybe because they took cues from Benny and acted more like dogs than cats) stole our hearts and taught me that there is always some new aspect of God's creation to embrace if you just give it time.

Truthfully, cats present a problem with Jewish ritual that most dogs do not. The tzitzit, the fringes on my tallit, are a source of constant fascination for the cats and they have attempted to unravel them many times over the years. In addition, we have to account for their presence at all times while the candles are lit on the kitchen counter. But their quiet calm demeanor is often just the cure for stressful times. Truly, there is a place for each of God's creations in our world and in our hearts.

When Benny died at age 13, we were determined not to get another dog. That determination lasted all of four months.

The house wasn't the same without a dog and we found our new friend, Sami, whom we adopted from a local rescue group. Sami is a classic mutt: a mixture of beagle, German Shepherd, Corgi and, God only knows what else. All that matters to me is that when I walk in the door, she stands up on her hind legs, smiles and hugs me just like Snoopy did to Charlie Brown. Sami has brought the loyal love of a dog back into our house and we are all richer for it.

I mention our animals often in my writing and, in that spirit, I share two sermons in which our animal family members played a part. In this first piece, it might appear that Benny played only a minor role. However, the idea for this sermon about an often-overlooked aspect of our world that came to me during one of our walks.

THE NEGLECTED SENSE
ROSH HASHANA 2006

As we begin the Amida, the silent standing prayer, we say: Ado-nai Sifatay Tiftach, O Lord, open my lips and my mouth shall speak your praise.

Nachmanides interpreted it differently: "O Lord, open my boundaries and my mouth shall speak your praise." Help me, O God, to find meaning in something I might have missed along the way.

Today's sermon is dedicated to that idea.

I had originally thought to deliver a sermon which included a traditional text dedicated to each of the five senses. But as I started to write, I realized that one of the senses kept calling out, in the words of the Talmud, "dirshuni," "Make a midrash out of me. Interpret me. Spend more time on me. Delve into me more deeply. Let people hear more about me and realize how much I can inspire them."

It was then that I decided that I would dedicate this sermon to only one of the five senses, one which has a rich history in our traditional texts, one which can inspire us and move us in its own unique way, and the one which, in our society, is the most often overlooked, taken for granted, and even ridiculed. I speak, of course, of the sense of smell.

How important smell is to our lives, to our understanding of the world and, according to our tradition, to our faith as well. Jewish tradition is full of references to aroma as memory, as comfort, as challenge, as inspiration. For those of us who have grown a bit tired of hearing or seeing or tasting or even touching the same old Jewish things, I offer the idea that a year in which we pay closer attention and give more respect to the sense of smell can recharge our Jewish lives in unexpected ways.

To be sure, there are blessings to be said for interactions with our sense of smell and I would encourage you to learn those blessings and use them appropriately. But I want to speak more conceptually.

Let me share with you four "smell" stories based on characters in the book of Genesis and let me begin with the story about Isaac blessing his son Jacob.

Isaac is old and blind. He calls for his son Esau, the hairy, malodorous hunter, to bring him food so that he can give him his due blessing as the firstborn. Rebecca, the mother of Esau and his twin brother Jacob, overhears the plan and knows that she must substitute Jacob, the younger child and the one who fulfills her image of who should receive the blessing.

But she has to figure out a way to fool her blind husband. She gives Jacob food, dresses him up in hunter's clothes and gloves of animal hair, and sends him in to be blessed by his father.

Apparently, though, she did not tell Jacob to imitate Esau's voice and so Isaac is confused and he says: hakol kol Ya'akov, vhayadayim yiday Esav – "The voice is the voice of Jacob but the hands are the hands of Esav." The old man is being betrayed by his senses. He can't see. He can't trust either his ears or his hands since they are sending opposite messages. The food is the same and taste won't affect the blessing. While the hairy clothes seem to help persuade him, the final criterion of identification is smell: "Behold," he says, "the smell of my son is like the smell of the field," and he blesses him.

Smell saves the day and Jacob receives the blessing. But the midrash says that there is more behind this than meets the eye – or the nose.

A midrash teaches that the "field" that Isaac smelled and that led him to identify the son standing before him as Esau was not the field of the hunt. Instead, the legend goes, Isaac smelled the Garden of Eden. He smelled paradise. He knew by this smell that the one before him was the one who deserved the blessing. It is because it is the smell of paradise that Isaac trusts in it and allows it to dictate the proper action.

How does the midrash arrive at the idea that he smelled the Garden of Eden?

*It is because, according to the rabbis, smell is the only pure and unblemished sense. When Eve ate from the fruit in the Garden of Eden, four of the five senses are mentioned as part of the sin: she **listened** to the snake, she **saw** the good fruit, she reached out to **take** it and she **tasted** it. The only sense not mentioned of the five is the sense of smell. It was not involved in the sin. Thus, a smell of paradise is as close as we can get to Eden, and when Isaac smells it, he knows that the blessing is going to its rightful recipient, one who can bring the world closer to returning to the garden.*

This passing aroma of Eden symbolizes the criterion we should use in judging how to act in a particular situation. It is our Jewish version of the expression that something has to pass the "smell test." If we are contemplating an action and, while doing so, catch a glimpse of a better world, through whatever sense it reaches us, we should act on it and help repair the world. We need to learn a lesson from this midrash and make judgments on our actions based upon how these actions can reflect the purity, the holiness, the divine within us and within our world. Whichever of our senses we use, let us seek out the original, the divine, the holy in all of our actions.

Then, there is the story of Noah. What finally convinces God to swear never to destroy the earth again, never to curse the world again because of the actions of human beings? It is the sweet smell of the sacrifices that Noah offers upon leaving the Ark. Vayarach Ado-nai et rayach hanichoach. "God smelled the sweet aroma of the sacrifices," and it reminded God of all that had been invested in human beings and God vowed never again to destroy them.

Scientists tell us that smell is the sense most closely related to memory and to the emotional impact memories can provide. Diane Ackerman notes in her book, A Natural History of the Senses: "Nothing is more memorable than a smell. One scent can be unexpected, momentary, and fleeting, yet conjure up a childhood summer beside a lake in the mountains; another, a moonlit beach; a third, a family dinner of pot roast and sweet potatoes during a myrtle-mad August in a Midwestern town. Smells detonate softly in our memory like poignant land mines hidden under the weedy mass of years. Hit a tripwire of smell and memories explode all at once. A complex vision leaps out of the undergrowth."

When God smells the sweet smell of the offerings, God demonstrates a reality which is so familiar for all of us. It reminds us what it feels like when we remember something which has given us such pleasure in the past.

Who among us hasn't been moved to remember based on a smell? Perhaps it is perfume or aftershave. Perhaps it is the smell of the cooking of a particular dish, the unique and distinctive scent of a home. These all are such powerful reminders of people we love who are not with us physically or only in memory.

We remember places as well through smell. Our family loves traveling to the Sleeping Bear Dunes area in the northwestern corner of Michigan's lower peninsula. So much of this area reminds me of New England. I can even fool myself while standing on the shore of Lake Michigan that maybe it's the Atlantic Ocean ... and then I take that deep breath, with no salt air, it's not Gloucester or Cape Cod. If the smell is missing, it just isn't the same.

No less an authority on the importance of the senses, Helen Keller wrote: "The perfumes are powerful magicians being able to transport us through years that you lived." Smell is clearly one of the most powerful triggers of memory that we have, and while aroma might bring sadness and longing, it brings comfort as well. God is comforted by the smell of the sacrifices, remembers times gone by, and realizes this is, in fact, the world with the potential for perfection. For us, those smells are precious as are the memories they inspire.

So take a moment to ask yourself: what memories, through what Jewish smells, are you creating for your children and your grandchildren in your home? I think that we have gone overboard trying to eliminate the aromas and odors from our homes to the point where we have severed a potentially critical connection of memory for the next generation. So here is a plea for the New Year: "Bring back the smells."

Next, there is Abraham. Abraham is likened to many things in the midrash. One of the most beautiful metaphors is that he is similar to a vial of perfume which is so intensely aromatic that, once opened, it spread through the entire world. When Abraham began his journey, the container was opened and its aroma began to spread.

As we continue the legacy of Abraham, we continue to spread this beautiful aroma throughout the world through our actions.

Back when I was young, we sometimes drove through the Boston neighborhood of Dorchester, past the old Baker's Chocolate Factory which filled the air with the sweetest smell of roasting cocoa.

The Baker's factory closed in 1965; but for years afterwards when we would make that trip, that smell was still hanging in the air. Was it the power of suggestion? Perhaps it was. But it is more likely the permanent impact that this intense beautiful smell had on the environment.

The metaphor of Abraham as perfume reminds us that our kind and constructive acts need not be directly heard or directly seen in order to make a difference. Their impact can spread throughout the world like a beautiful aroma carried by a breeze far away from its source. Long after we have stopped doing what we are doing and long after we have left this earth, after the sight and sound of our actions have disappeared, something continues to influence this world, the impact will not be forgotten. The aroma will hang in the air just as did Abraham's actions in turning the world towards God.

Finally, I conclude with the story of Joseph. When, Joseph reveals himself to his brothers, it happens in the Torah portion called Vayiggash. The word: "Vayiggash" means: "And he (Judah) drew near." It is when Judah draws near that Joseph, who has heard him and seen him all along, suddenly is moved to tears. He asks his brother to come closer. Then, he asks all his brothers to come closer. Why? He already could see them and hear them. I am convinced he told them to come closer because he wanted to smell them. He wants to stand with them and feel like family again, and the most primal, the most lasting, the most intense of all of the senses that bring him closer to others would be smell. If we don't recognize that, it is because, and for many good reasons, our culture has asked that we mask those odors. But make no mistake, they are there.

As most of you know, we are animal lovers in our home. Our dog, Benny, has heard every one of my sermons long before anyone else has; and he always wags his tail in approval. While I go on babbling, he goes on his own way during our walk interacting with his environment through the sense of smell. He is guided by smell to know what is his and what is not, what is lasting and what is fleeting.

When Joseph is surrounded by his family, he realizes what he has missed all of these years. I think the Torah is urging us to recognize, in whatever lasting way we can, that which is ours and that which we have missed; whether it is a place or a person, that aroma urges us to grab hold and hold on as long as we can.

Smell is associated with the most basic and most essential of all human activities: breathing. It is the sense which most surprises us, evoking memories, inspiring a love for people and places, spreading throughout the world a beauty and a plea for interaction that cannot go unnoticed.

This year, may we say: "O Lord, open up our noses to the smells of our beautiful world and help us to speak words of praise." May we be blessed with a year of wonderful smells, from fresh cut grass to bread baking in an oven, to the clean air after a spring shower. But may we also recognize in all the smells we experience the challenge to embrace this world and bring it back to paradise, where all fragrance is beautiful.

To conclude this chapter in honor of our animals, I offer you a sermon that was inspired by a rather unfortunate and potentially embarrassing typo that appeared in a local paper. I was more than willing to graciously turn that error into a tribute to all of the animals who make our lives and our world so much more meaningful:

THE RABBIT SPEAKS
1998

*Being in the public eye, rabbis are accustomed to occasional embarrass-ment and learn to take things good-naturedly. So I was much less em-barrassed than many thought I would be when a recent article in a local newspaper identified me, through a classic typographical error, as **Rabbit** Dobrusin. It gave my family a good laugh and I just brushed it off with a laugh and a wiggle of my nose.*

The timing of this error was rather interesting as I was teaching a class on the book of Psalms at the time and it inspired me to take a different approach in understanding my favorite Psalm.

Of all of the 150 Psalms, Psalm 8 is my favorite. In Psalm 8, the Psalmist says: "When I behold the heavens, the work of Your fingers, what is the hu-man being that You have regard for him?...yet you have made the human being a little lower than the angels and crowned him with glory and honor."

This statement clearly points to the paradox of the human being. We are so insignificant compared to the universe around us and yet, our uniqueness is clear. We are truly: "a little lower than the angels."

As I consider that statement, I try to imagine the setting that prompted the Psalmist to write these words. Many thoughts came into to my mind. The Psalmist was outside at night, when the heavens could be seen. There is a baby someplace either inside asleep (finally!) or awake in the Psalmist arms. This moved him to say: "From the mouths of infants and sucklings, You have founded strength." There is no better way to understand the paradox of the human condition than to hold an infant; so physically insignificant and yet so full of potential.

Then, I thought of one more aspect of the scene. The Psalmist must have been standing there with his dog. Of course, it could have been any animal from a cat to, dare I say, a rabbit. But the dog who shares our home with us would have it no other way than to have it be a loyal canine.

I put the dog into the picture because animals of all kinds, in all of their roles in our lives, play a special part in our understanding of who we really are.

One of those roles is mentioned specifically in the Psalm. The Psalmist includes a reference to all of the animals that are placed "at our feet," presumably to use for clothing and food. In Jewish tradition, animals are not the equals of human beings, far from it. Therefore, we are allowed the use of animals. But we are taught that there is sanctity to all forms of life and we are commanded to consider the pain of animals and to do our best to treat them with the respect that any form of life deserves.

There is another side to animals that the Psalmist does not mention but which I infer by my picture of the loyal dog standing by his side. I refer to those animals that we take into our hearts and into our homes, who stand by us and guard us through the night, who add one more element to our appreciation of the marvelous world which God has given us. When we consider the world and do so while scratching the ears of our dogs, cats, or any other furry animal, we see one more dimension to our lives and one more reason to praise God.

I imagine the Psalmist looking at the stars, cradling her infant, and realizing how great a world God has created, right down to the trusting relationship that exists between two such different and yet such similar creations: the human being and the animal.

Our children have been granted many blessings. Obviously, sharing our lives with our loyal four-legged friends is not the most important one. But we try to keep in mind that growing up with one of God's other creations in the house has given our children an additional insight into the majesty of the universe and the greatness of our Creator. It has helped them to laugh, to cry, and to understand love in one of its most basic forms. It is truly a blessing and I wouldn't have it any other way.

Our lives have been enriched and our days have been brightened by the presence of these loving creatures in our home. And here I have to mention, as well, the joy and the sweetness that Mickie's pet rats have brought to our home.

As we ponder what it means to be a Jew and what it means to be a human being, we should make sure to bring along the dog (or the cat or the rat), and understand better the gift of love with which we have been created. Make sure to get up right now and give that loyal friend a hug or a scratch – it will make their day – and yours.

8

Growing Up and Staying Young

Traditional Jewish texts are full of wisdom and much of it comes in unexpected places. Take for example this simple expression found throughout rabbinic literature as an instruction on how to read sacred text: *ayn mukdam u'miuchar baTorah*, "there is no "earlier and later" in the Torah." Simply put: the most important stories are not always told in chronological order.

When we seek to tell the story of our lives, the personal Torah each and every one of us is in the process of writing, this admonition is worth remembering. Sometimes, the best way to tell a story is to break out of the expectation that everything must related sequentially. Sometimes a bit of perspective and retrospective fills in the picture more clearly.

That explains why I've waited until now to write in detail about my teenage and college years.

As you would expect, my life was not a "black hole" between my days as a child playing baseball in front of our cottage and my years as a "grown up" rabbi. Something did come in between.

We all might like to forget our adolescent years. They can be the most difficult and painful of times. But an honest appraisal of how we came to be who we are today cannot ignore them.

Adolescent years are supposed to be times of rebellion but my teenage rebellions were boring and unremarkable in many ways. Still, I can't tell the story of my life as a rabbi without giving all the not-so-gory details.

I could have told the story earlier but I've delayed telling them until now because, in some sense, those adolescent stories are still being written.

To begin, I'll go back to a time before I reached those dreaded teenage years.

As I am sure is obvious by now, I was born and raised in Boston. I love the city and I love New England. As I get older, I find myself increasingly nostalgic for the "local" things I grew up with: candlepin bowling, or "regular bowling" as we so provincially called it, onion rings which were thin strings rather than thick slices and our favorite local TV "cowboy" show, Rex Trailer's Boomtown, just to name a few.

I'm sure anyone who has passed 40 can relate when I lament the fact that some things from my youth have gone the way of all of the earth. But some things do remain more or less the same and, during recent trips to Boston, I've found that they still play candlepins and the onion rings (at least the real ones) are still thin.

But among those people and places that I remember from my youth, there are some that have not survived the decades, and Rex Trailer is one of them. He died in 2013.

I will never forget him.

I had continued to watch Rex Trailer and his beautiful horse Goldrush for more years than most kids my age. I can still sing the theme song by heart (admit it: if you're a Bostonian of a certain age, you can too) and remember so much of the shtick.

So several years ago, right around my 50th birthday, I visited the Boomtown nostalgia website and saw that Rex Trailer was selling a DVD with highlights from the show. I wrote for it and included in my order a short message to Rex. I told him in my email that I was a rabbi. I also told him that one of my biggest childhood disappointments was that I wasn't selected to be the Sheriff when we went to see a taping of Boomtown.

He wrote me a lovely note back and in it he told me that I shouldn't be upset as I had a "higher calling."

I am not exaggerating when I say how thrilling it was to read that. How often does one have his career choice validated by a childhood hero? But after the euphoria settled down, reality set in. I stared at that email for what seemed like an eternity. Were we all really that old? Was that curly haired kid with the shy smile joining the "Boomtown Posse" and marching through the door of the Sherriff's office really me? How could it be so many years?

Whether I want to admit it or not, it *has* been so many years and Boomtown has been off the air for decades and that just shows you that not everything is the same as it used to be. There are things that aren't there anymore and can only be accessed by our own memories and the images and reminiscences occasionally available on the Internet.

As I think back on my childhood, I recall so many memories of places long-gone from the scene. Among these are the restaurants we frequented: Simeone's, a neighborhood Italian restaurant in Cambridge; the Clam Box, for onion rings and french fries not far from our cottage in Winthrop; and, Jack and Marion's, the New York style deli on Harvard Street, the center of our Jewish community.

Jack and Marion's is long since gone, and with it the huge cases of fancy dessert cakes and menus which were so big you could hardly pick them up. But Harvard Street is still there and while many of the businesses have gone the way of Rex Trailer and the Clam Box, there are still reminders on that street of my years growing up and how big a part that area played in my Jewish upbringing. It is a part of my life that I have been able to share with our kids and for that I am very grateful. While Ann Arbor has a wonderful Jewish community, it isn't like that of Boston (or New York or Chicago for that matter). But I wonder if anywhere today is quite like it was. Things have gotten far too complicated.

Even though there were synagogues that were closer to our house, we belonged to Congregation Kehillath Israel on Harvard Street. My father's family had belonged there and the Hebrew school was the best in the area. It was a great school to be sure and, leaving all of the inevitable Hebrew school wisecrack comments aside, my teachers there made an indelible impression on me.

Most of those impressions, even if I was too young to fully appreciate them, were positive and nurturing. But there is one teacher who especially stands out in my mind: Harry Kraft, may his memory be for a blessing, who was a larger-than-life presence to me and countless other kids at our synagogue.

Mr. Kraft was the epitome of a Jewish elder and I recognized this even when I was in elementary school. He would stand over us during our children's services, pointing to the words on the page of the prayer book, raising his deep voice to encourage us to sing and leading us in melodies which I still use when leading the service today.

With Mr. Kraft in control, everything seemed so safe and so predictable. That is one of the powers of ritual. Sitting in a service as a ten-year-old with a trusted figure at the head led me to believe that this was the way it was and always would be.

But Judaism cannot be only predictable. Sometimes it has to throw us a curve ball, and it did for me on Tuesday afternoon, November 9, 1965.

How can I remember the date so precisely? If you lived in Boston or anywhere in the Northeastern US at that time, you will always remember that day.

November 9, 1965, was the date of the first great power blackout in the Northeast. When the lights went out during Hebrew school, our teacher, a lovely sweet older woman who had lived through blackouts during World War II in Europe was suddenly and cruelly thrust back into those days.

We saw a side of her we had never seen: fear, dread, and the pain of memories of violent anti-Semitism. She screamed and pleaded with us to hide in the closet or under our desks. It was a very upsetting experience for our class and as I told the story to my parents that evening as we sat at a candlelit dinner table, I did so with more than a bit of confusion and maybe even anger. I felt I had missed out on something.

My teacher's panic attack had given me a sense that I had never had of the realities that many Jewish families face as memories of anti-Semitism and of the Holocaust arise. It was something I knew nothing about for my parents never discussed it in our presence.

For my parents, Judaism was never a source of sadness or fear. We weren't lectured as children about how anti-Semitism was prevalent in the world. We weren't taught that Judaism was about pride in being a Jew in contrast to others in the world. We were taught that Judaism was a religious faith and while we were expected to remain committed to our Jewishness, we were taught that Judaism was about being a mentsch and living with others peacefully, and we were taught that others would reciprocate.

The next day, when my teacher explained to us why she reacted as she had, it opened my eyes to something that I had never seen. Suddenly, even at that age, it occurred to me that maybe there *was* danger out there for Jews and that not everyone grew up in the privileged environment I had. But since it hadn't been part of my earliest lessons about Judaism, I wondered where it all fit in.

A day or so after the blackout, I had forgotten the whole issue, but it has never been too far beneath the surface. I still am trying to make sense out of the role that the fear and pride and "otherness" of being a Jew fits into the idealistic, universalistic approach to Judaism to which I am committed today.

But back in the mid 1960s, if there were any internal struggles going on in the minds of Jews, you would have never known it on Harvard Street. We were surrounded by friends who didn't lecture us about Jewish identity and didn't engage in controversial discussions about Jewish life. They just had Shabbat dinner, went to and from shul, and ran their businesses.

The "Jewish" stores on Harvard Street were unforgettable. There was the fish market with its unique smell and the big fish in neon lights in the window; the kosher butcher shop with its men in bloody aprons and the sawdust covered floors; the appetizer store with its whitefish "chubs" and more exotic species; the bakeries with their black and white cookies and "coffee rolls"; the deli, where I would later work as a waiter during high school and where I learned significant "people skills" that would help me repeatedly in the rabbinate; the Jewish supermarket, with its open boxes of macaroons and marshmallow candies sold by the pound at Pesach time; the Jewish book stores with volumes containing serious academic works and, in general, a much less preachy and much less dogmatic approach to Judaism and Jewish life than you might find in such stores today.

But the most important of all the stores on Harvard Street was Irving's Toy and Card Shop.

While Irving's sold little toys, soda (or "tonic" as Bostonians called it), greeting cards, newspapers and other such things, the product they sold that most interested me and my friends was penny candy.

Irving's occupied a space directly across Harvard Street from the Hebrew school entrance, and every day before school we would cross the street and Abe or Ethel would let us "regulars" step around the counter and pick our own candy from the cabinet and then trusted us to give them an accurate count.

It may not sound like much but it helped make going to Hebrew school tolerable and, more than that, it was another introduction to this young Jew of the meaning of ritual in our lives. It is, I'm sure, not surprising to hear that a Squirrel Nut Chew or an Atomic Fireball was more significant to me in those days than any of the ritual items of the synagogue, even when Mr. Kraft was showing us how to properly use them.

Going to Harvard Street was, in and of itself, a ritual. It didn't matter if the goal was to go to shul or to buy chicken, to pick up the dry cleaning, or go to a funeral. It was our home and, as I think back on those days, I realize that it was on that street that I learned what it meant to live in a Jewish community. In those days, you just had to walk down the street three or four times a week and it seemed you understood what it meant to be a Jew.

However, as I approached my teens in the late 1960s, America became a much more complicated place. That is the world I entered as a bar mitzvah when suddenly the picture on the street and in my heart and soul wasn't so clear.

Robert Dobrusin

As I grew through high school, I found that Harvard Street seemed to get smaller and my questions about what it meant to be a Jew grew larger. I vacillated between becoming more observant and walking away entirely.

It is in that context that I rebelled for the first time. I wouldn't call it a full-scale rebellion, but in this small way I was trying to move a bit from the path my parents had set for me and the path that my friends and their older brothers and sisters had taken. I decided that I wanted to attend our synagogue's two-day-a-week high school program instead of the more intensive high school program at the Boston Hebrew College which all the "serious students" from our synagogue attended. And, I had a good reason.

In order to attend the program at Hebrew College on a reasonable schedule during the school year, you had to attend five mornings a week during the summer. But after one summer of attending those classes, I realized that it wasn't for me. I had something else in mind. During the summer of 1970 as idealism raged throughout Boston and other student communities, I wanted to volunteer at a hospital.

I argued with my parents that if Judaism was about being a good person, this is how I intended to be a better person, and it made infinitely more sense to me to volunteer than to sit in a classroom four hours a day. Also, since I was planning on becoming a doctor, it was obviously more important for my future.

My parents were in a tough spot because, while they admired my idealism, they knew that meant I would not be able to go back to Hebrew College during the school year and this might not look right. So, we sought a compromise with the school, but they stood firm. If I wanted to go to Hebrew College during the year on a reasonable schedule, I would have to go during the summer. It seemed so unfair. At the time, I didn't understand why Jewish education shouldn't be just like stepping behind the candy counter at Irving's and taking what I wanted. Today, as a rabbi of a synagogue, I think I understand better why we need standards and expectations, but each time I think about it seriously, I think of taking what I wanted at the penny candy store and I pause and shake my head.

The result was that, with my parents' blessing, I walked away from traditional Jewish study and enrolled in a more participatory and, truthfully, more meaningful program for me.

It may not seem like much of a rebellion but I carry that memory with me to this day because that minor rebellion taught me something. It was the moment that insured that Judaism would continue to have personal meaning for me and was a small step towards independence.

Through it all, my Jewish identity remained firm. Most of my free time was spent at the synagogue with my friends at services and in our youth group. But as college loomed on the horizon, the questions arose again. My dream was to go to a small college in a small country town in New England, even if it didn't have a significant Jewish community.

This time, my parents were less enthusiastic about my idealistic visions while I remained adamant. But at the urging of some of my teachers and the rabbi in the small synagogue in one of those towns who, upon seeing what being Jewish meant to me, begged me NOT to go to the local college, I decided to follow in my brother's footsteps, to attend Brandeis University.

Shortly after I started at Brandeis, away from home for the first time, I realized what a good decision it was. I needed that Jewish community around me and relished the one I found at Brandeis. There I was able to struggle, along with some close friends, with the thoughts of what I really wanted to be as a Jew.

Brandeis was the site of my second rebellion, one of which Mr. Kraft, I assume, would never have approved. It seemed logical that my first stop at Brandeis would be the Orthodox minyan each Shabbat morning as it was relatively close to what I was accustomed. Except for the *mechitza*, separating the men and women during prayer, it was just like our Junior Congregation services at our traditional Conservative shul.

After attending the Orthodox service for the first couple of weeks, I heard that there was another service on campus – with all of the traditional prayers and even some of Mr. Kraft's melodies – but with one major change. It was "egalitarian": women and men participating equally, something that never would have happened at KI.

I took a deep breath and went one Shabbat morning and immediately found that community to be exactly what I was looking for – it seemed completely natural to me. However, I will never forget the look on my father's face when he came to services on parents' weekend during my freshman year and saw a woman reading from the Torah.

My father actually argued with me on this one and while I don't remember what I said, I'd like to think that it was like a scene I remember from a particularly emotional episode of *All in the Family* in which Mike is arguing with Archie about racial equality and Archie references his father's teaching him about differences between the races. Finally, Mike says: "Archie, your father was wrong, your father was wrong." Archie can't accept it but Mike stood strong and I spoke strongly that day.

While he did come to grudgingly accept it, I can't blame my father for not immediately embracing the equality of women in synagogue life. But I can blame him and his contemporaries for giving us such a hard time about following our hearts. I'd like to think that has made me and others of my generation more willing to understand our kids' priorities and allowing them freedom to move away from our way of doing things. Maybe, anyway...

By the middle of my senior year, and to no one's surprise except perhaps my own, I made the decision to apply to rabbinical school. I wasn't sure but it was worth a try. Even as my days at Brandeis came to an end, I still wasn't convinced that it was the right decision for me, and I wasn't sure I would ever really finish the long road to ordination. That uncertainty remained until one day, a few months after my graduation from Brandeis, when I realized I had made precisely the right decision.

The story of that day began one afternoon in mid-June. The market for student summer jobs in 1977 was tough and I had not found work yet. I was sitting at home probably looking through airline timetables when I got a phone call from a close friend who asked what I was doing for the summer. When I told her that I hadn't found a job yet, she told me what I was going to do: "You're coming to Camp Ramah to be a counselor."

I was very familiar with Camp Ramah, the educational camp of the Conservative Movement, as my brother had been a staff member at one of the camps for years. But I had always resisted the idea of going to camp as a kid and wasn't that much more comfortable with the idea as a college graduate. I hesitated, stammered, and thought of excuses but she persisted. They were short of staff. I needed a job. Besides, she said: "With all due respect to rabbinical school, this is where you will really learn to be a rabbi."

So with no more excuses and with my parents hoping beyond hope I would get out of the house that summer, I threw caution to the wind and a couple of days later, I drove myself to Palmer, Massachusetts.

I arrived at camp and I took one last deep breath before driving down the narrow road up to the office. At that moment, I could never have envisioned how much it would mean to me in later years to drive down that same road for the first time each summer, returning after 10 months of "exile" to the place that became "home" for me. At that time, though, it was all unknown territory and it became treacherous unknown territory when, a few minutes after arriving, I was told that the next day I would meet 14 thirteen-year-olds who would be my and my co-counselor's responsibility for the summer. I almost turned around and left.

I'm forever grateful that I didn't.

As the summer began, I felt like I was as much of a camper as my 7th graders. Thanks to some of my fellow staff members, most of whom were more experienced at camp than I was, I was able to learn the ropes, although it wasn't always pretty. Like any city kid that goes to camp out in the woods, I began to learn skills that I had never known before. I learned how to paddle a canoe, I learned some rudimentary first aid, and I learned how to start a campfire. By the way, I've only done that once since then – with Avi when he was five and we went out camping for a night. Somehow, with Avi watching so carefully, I was successful. It must have been divine intervention.

But in addition, I learned something else. I learned how to be a teacher and, therefore, as my friend had promised, I learned how to be a rabbi.

I learned how to take advantage of teachable moments, how to comfort and how to challenge, how to use Jewish texts to help people respond to situations around them, how to set priorities and stick by them.

I began to realize that if we can't create a perfect Jewish community at least we can create a very positive one, and that the key is the values on which we build that community. I look back to what I experienced at Camp Ramah and realize that, just as my parents taught me more than "Jewish pride," more than any sense of "chosen-ness" or "superiority," what Jews need is to be part of a community with values they can be proud of – kindness, compassion, and seeking and pursuing peace.

I learned those lessons at camp. Sometimes I learned them the hard way. I made mistakes and missed opportunities that bothered me terribly and still do. But I also remember the successes that still mean the world to me more than 30 years later.

As much as I learned from my colleagues, I learned more from my campers as I watched them go through the struggles of adolescence. It was then that I realized for the first time since my bar mitzvah that I was still a kid. I was still growing, still struggling, and that working with these children was helping me clarify some of my own thoughts.

On the day camp ended and the kids left, I heaved a deep sigh of relief and then I started to cry a bit. I have never forgotten that moment. I mourned for what I had lost now that camp was over and realized that I could find more of that every day in the rabbinate. It was that day, two weeks before I started rabbinical school, that I decided that I really wanted to be a rabbi.

I went back to camp year after year and yearned for the chance to create a synagogue which would reflect some of what I had learned at camp.

The fact that I worked with 13-year-olds that first summer and for several years after helped me understand the importance of that age. I still find myself treasuring the opportunities I have to work with kids of bar/bat mitzvah age. I find that the questions these kids ask, as well as the ones they don't, are the most critical questions we face as Jews and as human beings. I can honestly say that my greatest gratification as a congregational rabbi occurs when one of these kids, now in college or beyond, contacts me to ask a question about an issue of concern to them.

The experience of being asked those questions years later made me realize something critical and I spoke about it one year on the second day of Rosh Hashanah:

THE "IN-BETWEEN" DAY AND OUR "IN-BETWEEN" LIVES
ROSH HASHANA 2005

On the first day of Rosh Hashanah, we are like children, finding wonder in even the simplest aspect of the holiday. Everything looks and feels new and exciting.

On Yom Kippur, we are mature adults, completely aware of the seriousness of the day, confronting the most "grown up" of thoughts as we consider the sad reality that we have fallen short of our aspirations and must confront our mortality.

So where does that leave us on the second day of Rosh Hashanah? If we are children on the first day of Rosh Hashanah and adults on Yom Kippur, then the second day of Rosh Hashanah leaves us all feeling like adolescents. We're not as excited on the second day as we were the day before when everything was new. Like teenagers we know something more important lies ahead, and while we can't wait for it to come, we're not really sure we'll be ready for it.

So this morning, on this in-between day, let me speak about adolescence.

My interest in this entire issue is inspired by my own experience working with adolescents but is also inspired by a great story that was publicized not long ago: the story of sixteen-year-old Keron Thomas. You may not remember his name, but Keron Thomas pulled off one of the greatest adolescent pranks in history. He lived in New York City and loved subways. He read about them, studied all of the maps and all of the driver's manuals, and one day he put to use all of the knowledge that he had accumulated over the years pursuing his passionate interest. He masqueraded as a conductor, stood in line with other drivers, picked up the keys and drove an A train full of passengers from Brooklyn through Manhattan. It was only when he went a little too fast around a curve that an investigation turned up the truth.

It was terribly dangerous prank and Keron Thomas was punished and deservedly so. But he became a folk hero to many because of his daring creativity. As one who also loves subways, I thought of how I reflected that love: by looking out the front window of the car. Keron Thomas had chutzpah I never had and part of me kept thinking: Kol Hakavod, good job!

It is dangerous to steal subway cars, and thank God most of us don't do it or anything like it. But somewhere deep inside, we would love to pursue our craziest dreams. In fact, we are all struggling with the issues of growth and change, with the disappointments of failure, with the awkwardness of being a human being. Today and every day, we have great dreams that we can't quite seem to fulfill, but, oh, how we would love to try!

Today and every day, somewhere deep inside, we are all adolescents.

That fact is critical for us as Jews. It's good we've grown up from childhood because Judaism is not a religion for kids. Of course, we have to teach our children about Judaism and help them to see its importance, but in the end, kids just won't get it.

Judaism is not really a religion for grown-ups either. When we stop growing, when we reach a point where we're not interested in change any more, when we have stopped struggling with the world and stopped dreaming greater things, Judaism begins to lose its purpose.

So no matter whether you're celebrating the 1st anniversary of your bar or bat mitzvah, the 37th as I did this year or the 87th, Judaism demands of you that you still see yourself as growing, changing, struggling, developing, and seeking ways to make an impression on the world. While the world might seem largely disinterested in you, sometimes we can make the world pay attention.

Judaism is, therefore, the perfect religion for all of us adolescents. It is a faith for those who find the world to be a frustrating, perplexing place: so large at times that we seek a place to hide, so small at times that we seek a way to stretch our wings. It is a faith for those who feel so independent at times that we scoff at the idea of needing anyone or anything to guide us, and so dependent at times that we'd gladly go back to elementary school if someone would let us in. It is a faith for those who are willing to dream, knowing that all will not be achieved. It is a faith for those with more questions than answers, more doubt than certainty, for those who believe tomorrow will be better even though it seems so far off. It is a faith for growing, changing human beings. It is a religion for all of us adolescents.

We are most familiar with adolescence in Jewish tradition through bar and bat mitzvah. When a new Jewish "adult" stands on this bima, we bless him or her with a blessing which expresses the hope that he or she will, among other things, be shalaym with God. The word shalaym, root of the word shalom, means complete and it is translated in our siddur as: May she be wholehearted in her faith.

I love the phrase but I do not like the translation. I need a new one. Sometimes my heart just isn't whole and I am glad for that because it means I am struggling with critical questions. So what can we mean when we tell our children to be "wholehearted in their faith"?

There is no doubt that in some of the sources in which this phrase occurs, it means just what it appears to mean: complete, wholehearted, unshaken, with an unchanging faith in God. But in the struggles of our daily lives, amidst the nagging questions that arise, in the adolescent-like wavering between being all-powerful and completely impotent, such permanent faith is hard to come by. It is, in the long run, I believe, detrimental to our lives.

There is a phrase in the Torah which seems to have inspired this line in the blessing. Following his reunion with his brother Esau, the Torah says; "Vayaytzay Ya'akov Shaleym": Jacob left whole, complete..

Rashi says that Jacob was shaleym begufo, shaleym bitorato, shaleym bimamono, complete in body, complete in Torah, complete in possessions.

This is strange because Jacob had reason to have big gaps in all three areas. Complete in body? He had injured his thigh in his wrestling match *with the angel. Complete in Torah? He couldn't have found the time to study Torah during his years of wandering and working for his father-in-law Laban. Complete in possessions? He had just given Esau many of his own possessions as a gift in order to appease him.*

Rashi knew these questions and he had answers. Jacob was complete in body because his injury had healed. He was complete in Torah, because he suddenly remembered all of the Torah he had forgotten. He was complete in his possessions because even though he had given away the gifts, he somehow magically found his possessions to be complete again.

But in this case, Rashi is living in a dream world, a world of simplicity, a world of children.

Shaleym bigufo? Complete in body? As we grow, we learn that some wounds never heal completely. We go through life the best we can and, God willing, do quite well. But the deepest wounds never completely heal.

Shaleym Bitorato? Complete in Torah? As we grow, we learn that the time which we have wasted along the way can not be magically made up.

Shaleym Bimamono? Complete in possessions? As we grow, we learn that we do not always get in return that which we give and the most important gifts are the gifts that do not come back to us.

So, I am uncomfortable with Rashi's claim that Jacob walked away from these critical moments of his life unchanged, unshaken, and unburdened by any sense of regret or pain or loss. I believe that it is unreasonable for our tradition to ask of us that we be shalaym with God if shalaym means forgetting everything that ever was negative or lacking in our relationship with God.

Jacob, the wrestler, the schemer, the dreamer, the great visionary, was once the prototypical adolescent. As he limps away from his intense interactions, having grown tremendously and having matured greatly, we can't assume that he has left behind all of his doubts, his pain, his struggles. How boring we would be and how meaningless our lives if all of our problems could be solved this easily.

Of course, each of us, and some more than others, can easily find an experience or two in our lives which we would dearly love to have never experienced. I understand that and do not mean to glorify or gloss over or even assume a higher purpose in pain or loss. But to envision a human life without a reasonable amount of conflict and loss and disappointment is not realistic, at least it is not the life that our tradition envisioned.

So I have to respectfully disagree with Rashi. I do not want our bar and bat mitzvah celebrants or the rest of us adolescents to think that being shalaym means wholehearted in our faith. For much of our lives, some or all of our heart will find it difficult to approach God with faith and serenity.

It happens to all of us and it even happens to rabbis. There are days I wake up in the morning and say: "How can I really believe all of this?"

At those moments, I don't have any thoughts of what lies beyond our world or what meaning my life might have or what is right and wrong or what some being I've never seen expects of me. At those moments, I am content to just plunk myself down on a chair and watch a ballgame during every free moment I might have and shut the rest of the world out.

This past summer I had one of those moments, in Jerusalem of all places! I was in Israel to participate in a serious Torah study program with some outstanding teachers in the best of all possible settings. One morning, as I gathered my material for 8 hours of Torah study, it suddenly dawned on me: "What am I doing with my life? Does any of this really matter? Do I really believe in this God I talk about? Why not just take the bus up to Tel Aviv or into the Galilee and do some hiking, or make the trip to Jordan I've always wanted to take? Why spend my day studying Torah?" I sat down in my chair in my hotel room, closed my eyes and thought and in a few minutes, I realized how to translate this phrase: being shalaym with God.

For in those few minutes, as I sat and thought about these questions, the loneliness that I felt being away from my family got so much stronger and so much more difficult. I wanted to go home. Then I realized that there was a greater loneliness I was feeling, even in that brief time.

That is when the new translation of this phrase hit me. To be shalaym with God doesn't have to mean to be "wholehearted in one's faith." It can mean to understand that my life is only shalaym, only complete, with God. Without a creator, without a lawgiver, without a redeemer, my life is not complete. My life is not complete without God to praise, to question, to shake my fist at, to be inspired and challenged by. My life is not complete unless I feel that there is a being for whom I, and all of those around me, are the ultimate hope of a yet unfinished dream.

But my vision, my opinion, my job approval rating of God changes from one day to the next. I can even turn my back on God every once in a while, knowing that when I turn back God will be there. But when I do I turn my back, I am subject to that terrible loneliness, lost in a world suddenly much too big … or much too small.

In return, I believe that what God wants from us is to be the best we can be as human beings, and that means that we will be full of conflict and doubt and struggles and dreams and hopes and cynicism and the constant balance between being the center of the universe and a meaningless speck so far from the center that it can't even be seen.

We will settle some of those conflicts as we grow but, God forbid, if we ever think we've grown up enough to figure them all out, we're in serious trouble because then we won't need God anymore and, how incomplete, how non-shalaym, our lives would be!

As has been said many times by many people of many faiths, God is not here to answer all of the questions. God is here to remind us what the questions are. God is not here to make our lives easy. God is here to help us through the pain that is inevitable in life.

In conclusion, then, let me return to the analogy of the adolescent.

There is not a parent in the world who can answer all of their adolescent's questions. All they can do is to be there, at times distant to allow for growth, at times as close as close can be for their child to hold on tight, to assure their bar or bat mitzvah, their new adult still finding his or her way, that even though they may shed some tears, there is a better day on the horizon. In the meantime, they tell them to enjoy their dreams, live to the best of their abilities, grace their days and their worlds through appropriately careful creativity to try to make their dreams reality. That is what God tells us every day – grab onto this world, love it, enjoy it, and find a way to make our mark.

An adolescent often turns his back on his parents imagining he can do better without them, but knows deep inside that his life would not be complete without them in it. So do we, in our successes, in our struggles, in our doubts, in our questions, in our celebrations, in our being true b'nai Yisrael, children of Jacob, the wrestler with God, know that, even if we stray, even if we become educated to the point at which it all seems silly, even if we replace the Divine with every idea or action or commitment we can find, our lives would simply not be shalaym without God.

More importantly, I believe with perfect faith, that God's existence is not shalaym without each and every one of us: for we are all God's adolescents whom God loves so dearly and holds so tightly even as we squirm to get away.

We are all adolescents. We are all struggling and wrestling with ideas, with emotions, with priorities. Whatever the subject, I believe that showing ourselves as wrestling is absolutely essential as rabbis. It isn't always well received by those who want Judaism to be more simple and clear, but it is the only way to keep our faith and our people growing.

We need to ask the difficult questions and resist being railroaded by anyone into denying that there are deep conflicts in the world we face as Jews. We need to read the newspapers as critically as we read the Torah. We need to speak up, aware of the history of our people, respectful of the fears and concerns of Jews who have been through different experiences than us, cautious to understand the big picture but always willing to speak our mind.

We need to confront our own selves as well.

A few years ago, on my 25th Rosh Hashanah in Ann Arbor, I delivered what was perhaps my most emotional sermon. It revealed what has been, for me, a source of the great tension that I referred to earlier in this chapter and have felt increasingly over the past years. It also demonstrated that, occasionally, we stand up after our wrestling matches more sure of who we are and more comfortable with ourselves.

Unlike most of the other sermons in this book, the "story" is not behind the sermon but contained in the sermon itself.

DARKNESS AND SUNSHINE
ROSH HASHANA 2012

Let me begin this morning with a verse from a song called Sunday Morning Sunshine, written by Harry Chapin. In many ways, it describes some of what I feel, looking back on my 25 years here in Ann Arbor:

> **"I came into town with a knapsack on my shoulder**
> **And a pocket full of stories that I just had to tell.**
> **You know I'd knocked around a bit and I'd had my share of small town glories.**
> **It was time to hit the city and that crazy carousel...**
> **These streets were never highways. I had not known the sky above.**
> **These days were never my days for I had not known your love.**
> **It's funny how a city can put on a different face. When it holds the one you care for.**
> **It becomes a different place**
> **You brought your Sunday Morning Sunshine here into my Monday morning world."**

I have grown to know and to love this community. It holds the ones I care for, all of you whom I have gotten to know over 25 years. And, of course, it holds the one whose love sustains me every day.

I did come into town with a pocketful of stories. Some were the classic rabbinic stories rabbis pick up along the way, but some were personal stories I chose to tell during classes or occasionally from the bima. Now, many years later, I have many more stories to share and today, I want to tell you the story of one of the most significant experiences of my life.

It is a story about darkness and a story about sunshine.

One Shabbat morning in January, I was at home, having taken that Shabbat off for vacation, when the doorbell rang. The mail carrier was at the door with a registered letter.

I had been expecting the letter. It was from the governmental archives of the nation of Latvia. A few months before, I had submitted a request for information about my paternal grandfather's family. My grandfather came to America from Latvia in 1907 and died when my father was a young man.

Our family had been fascinated with the history of the Dobrusins for decades and the search for information had been a true adventure. Despite significant effort, we were unable to find any meaningful information about the family until an extraordinary experience brought progress to our search for our roots.

Suddenly, one day, I received an email from a friend from college whom I hadn't been in contact with for 30 years telling me that she had just learned that her husband's maternal grandmother's maiden name was Dobrusin. She wondered if we might be related. It turned out her husband's grandmother was my grandfather's sister. We were second cousins. A rift in the family had occurred in the 1940s and there was very little contact between the first cousins for decades. Now, through this coincidence, second cousins one generation removed from the rift found each other and combined our knowledge about the family's past.

Then, in another extraordinary coincidence, I found out that a good friend's father had come from the same city of D'vinsk that my family had come from, and he knew exactly to whom I had to write to get the information I wanted.

And here the letter with that information was in my hand.

I sat for a few moments staring at it and then opened and began to read.

The letter contained the details of the family from the Russian census of 1897. It listed my great grandparents Itzik and Hilda, whose father's name was Hayim, apparently the one for whom my father was named. It listed four sons and daughters; Julius, my grandfather; and his two siblings, Annie and Louis, who also came to America. It noted their sister Rebecca who died at a young age in Latvia. The census records listed their occupations, education level, and even their street addresses in D'vinsk (now known as Daugavpils). Immediately I decided I had to go to Latvia and stand on those streets and see where I came from.

But something was missing. We knew there was another brother. We thought his name was Shael. Where was he?

I turned the page and found that, in fact, Shael and his family had moved to a different town. He had moved with his wife and children, one of whom, my father's first cousin, shared his name Hayim, to a town called Preili, 30 kilometers to the north. There, Shael lived with his wife Luba who was to die young, three children, their spouses, and three grandchildren.

So what happened to them? According to documents taken from the Soviet Archives of the 1940s, Shael, his children, and his grandchildren were all killed during the first days of the Nazi occupation of Latvia in a massacre of the Jews of Preili on August 9, 1941. All of them were murdered simply because they were Jews.

You might know of a TV program which deals with genealogical searches of celebrities called "Who Do You Think You Are?" At that moment, I realized my answer to that question "Who Do You Think You Are?" had forever changed. I could no longer say as I had said for years: "No one in my close family died in the Holocaust." In that one moment, the Shoah became more than a Jewish story. It was now **my family's story** and virulent anti-Semitism was not just a concept but was a family reality.

In the next months as I did more research, I learned quite a bit. First, I discovered that my great uncle's and cousins' deaths had been recorded at Yad Vashem, the Holocaust memorial in Jerusalem, and testimony was accessible on the Internet. Why hadn't we looked? No one in our family had thought to look at the records of Yad Vashem in searching for information about Shael. Were we escaping what we knew in our hearts to be true?

Those Yad Vashem records also contained the name of the man who had submitted the testimony concerning my family. He was a resident of Preili who was in the Russian army at the time of the massacre. He lived in Haifa, Israel and I found his phone number and called him. After a moment of hesitation, he spoke to me briefly and he acknowledged that he knew my family. He said: "Shael Dobrushin was the gabbai (the assistant to the rabbi) in the old shul in Preili."

When I heard him call my great-uncle by his name, I felt my knees begin to shake.

I also learned that there was a Holocaust memorial in the town of Preili, alongside the abandoned Jewish cemetery, the site of the massacre where my family members were slaughtered. The names of the victims were buried in a capsule under the monument and a bit more research assured me that my family's names were there.

At that moment, the focus of my planned trip became Preili. And one June day, after a four-hour train ride from the capital city of Riga and a 45-minute bumpy drive across the back roads of southeastern Latvia, I arrived in Preili.

As I walked from the car to the monument, a line from a movie suddenly came to my mind. It was an odd movie to think of at that time. It wasn't Schindler's List or any other Shoah movie. Rather, it was a line from the children's movie "Lilo and Stitch" which at one time was a favorite in our family. The movie features a comment on the Hawaiian word for family: "Ohana means family. Family means no one left behind or forgotten."

I thought of that line over and over again. My family members had been left behind. But now they would no longer be forgotten.

I walked up to the monument and performed the simple act of remembering: placing stones I had brought from Ann Arbor on the memorial. Then, I stood for a few moments in silence.

After those few moments, I found myself wanting to say something to Shael and his family and the words that came out of my mouth surprised even me. I said: "I am ashamed that in over 70 years no one from the family came to visit you. I apologize but I came as soon as I heard."

"I came as soon as I heard." Those were the words that came to me – words that we say to people when they think we haven't cared when in fact we didn't know. But sometimes we don't know because we don't try hard enough to know and, deep in my heart, I knew we had blinded ourselves for several decades. We should have known. Whether we knew the details or not, we should have realized what had happened to our family.

After saying the memorial prayer and walking around the abandoned cemetery for a few minutes, I left and, truthfully, if I had gone right back to the airport in Riga and had flown home, my trip would have been worthwhile. But I was in Latvia for another few days and so I visited Daugavpils, my grandfather's birthplace.

With the help of my guide and a local Jewish historian, I learned about the city, a place of great Jewish learning and serious intellectual debate. It was the town where my grandfather came to reject his family's Jewish tradition and embraced socialism and Zionism. It was the town where his eyes had been opened to seeing something more than the closed, shtetl-like Judaism of his father and his brother, the gabbai of Preili. It was the town from which he left to come to America, and that is exactly what occurred to me while standing on the street where the family lived in Daugavpils.

I didn't think to myself: "This is where he lived" but "This is the town he left." This is the town he escaped from to start a new life in America. After seeing what there was to see, I couldn't wait to join him in leaving.

It was a pleasant enough city and people were friendly, but it was not my place. There was no one and nothing there that made it my place. To paraphrase Harry Chapin: "Those streets were never my ways and I had not known this sky above."

I spent my second and last night in Daugavpils tossing and turning as voices I didn't recognize and didn't understand bounced around in my head. Some of this was brought on by the exhaustion of travel but it was more likely emotional turmoil as I felt as if my grandfather and all of the others who left like him were telling me to go home, back to America, the place they came to. I couldn't stop thinking about it or watching the clock. It was the longest, most unsettling night of my life. As much as I had needed to go to Daugavpils and as much as I was glad I had done so, that was how deeply I needed to leave.

It was raining when I boarded the early morning express train to Riga. I fell asleep almost immediately, a deep blessed sleep. I woke up when the train made its first stop an hour and a half later to see the sun shining. I smiled from ear to ear.

That day, Friday, was a great day. I thoroughly enjoyed Riga: a lovely city. The sun was shining. I went to the city's central market and on an architectural walking tour and basked in the sunshine of the city which was once called: "The Paris of the North."

On Shabbat morning, the sun was still shining when I went to the one active shul in Riga to say Kaddish for Uncle Shael and his family.

As I was settling into my seat, I looked around the synagogue and my eye was drawn to the Hebrew inscription around the Aron Kodesh. It shocked me. It wasn't the type of quotation you usually see above the ark, expressing spiritual yearning or simple faith. It was a verse from Psalms: "Blessed be God who did not abandon us to become prey for their teeth."

Being survivors defined this Jewish community's existence and I could not turn away from the inscription.

I focused on two Hebrew letters: nun and vav, "us," who did not abandon **us**. I asked myself: how had the knowledge I had gained in the past six months changed me? Who do I think I am? Am I part of that **us**?

In the sense that all Jews are intertwined, of course, we are all part of that " us". But beyond the platitudes, what does the story of my great uncle's death mean to me? Am I now, in some distant way to consider myself and my family as survivors? How does knowing the fact that there were more second cousins that I would never meet because they died in the most horrible ways imaginable affect who I am and how I see the world?

That was the key question for me. I started thinking: Does it still make sense to do what I have done more ardently as the years have gone along – embracing the liberal perspective of the late 20th century American Jewry I was raised in, with its idealistic attitudes that were influenced by freedom and comfort? Here I am working for interfaith causes, spending time on more global concerns, believing we can form alliances with people who used to hate us or still may. Here I am now serving as the co-chair of T'ruah: The Rabbinic Call for Human Rights, an organization which believes that high on our agenda as Jews must be addressing the human rights of all peoples throughout our country and throughout Israel and the territories? What do I say now that I am confronted with my family's history? Is this a path I have to reconsider? Can I be as positive about the future? Should I still find time to reach out beyond the Jewish world in the work that I do? Or do I think of my great-uncle and his family and focus entirely on the survival of our people knowing that the world stands against us and – that "if I am not for my-self who will be for me"?

Of course, I recognize that many who came out of the Shoah are dedicated to those same idealistic values and, in some cases, it was the experience of the Shoah which led them to those commitments. But it does seem obvious that the values of trust and idealism are easier to come by if you have not experienced such pain. I have been told very often by people in this congregation that I would likely feel differently about the world if my parents had been born in Europe or if I had sat in the lap or at the feet of those whose had suffered unthinkable harm at the hands of the Nazis. I know it is not true for all survivors or their children, but it is true for many that the pain and agony has led them, quite understandably, to be less open and trusting of others in the world. I understand and I acknowledge that. But how does this apply to me, and is the answer different than it was before I read the letter from Latvia and sat staring at the inscription in the Riga shul?

So I struggled with this question and tried to figure out where I fit in. I thought of what it means to grow up in freedom, what the benefits and potential dangers are. I thought of my parents, my teachers, my colleagues who have inspired me to fight against the apathy and selfishness that good fortune sometimes brings. Then, I thought of so many of my colleagues who see things so differently from me.

I spent several sleepless nights wrestling with these questions and after weeks and weeks of wrestling I came up with an answer.

I cannot change who I have come to be.

Of course, this experience will have an impact on my thinking. It will strengthen the obligation I already feel and hopefully share with all of you to respond to incidents or threats of anti-Semitism at home or elsewhere. I will, I assume, respond a bit more quickly as my words to Shael: "I came as soon as I heard" echo in my mind.

This experience will also further solidify my commitment to Israel as I was reminded again how much safer a world this is for Jews with a Jewish state.

But even though that is true, I still worry about linking Israel too strongly with the Shoah. It is not enough to think of Israel solely from the perspective of Yad Vashem. We have to think about Israel in other ways than just a response to or the prevention of another holocaust. Jewish survival is not enough. We need to think about the values we embrace, the way we live, what we do with our survival, and what we teach the world.

This trip didn't change how deeply I feel that. I am still an idealist.

Because my grandfather came to this great country, I have had the blessing of security which has given me a completely different set of experiences and a completely different perspective on what it means to be a Jew than Shael might have had.

So, ultimately, Shael's life and death will never be as great an influence on my life as the story of my grandfather Julius.

When Grandpa Dobrusin left Latvia, he left for a place where he could give his children and grandchildren a better life, a place where three generations later, we live safely as Jews in a multi-cultural, more universalistic society. I have grown up nurtured by that freedom and that dream. That *is who I am. And nothing, not even the tragic story of Shael's life is going to change that. Nor should it.*

I think of Mordecai Kaplan's words; "The past has a vote but not a veto."

My experience in Latvia will have a vote in how I view the world and my role as a Jew.

But it will not have a veto.

*Whether I am part of the "us" who was saved from the Holocaust could be debated. But what can't be debated is that I am part of the "us" whose life has been lived in freedom and comfort, and that has fostered in me to a set of priorities which I feel are critical and necessary for the Jewish people and for the world at large. Just as our people must hear with great reverence and respect the stories of those who have experienced anti-Semitism most directly to remind us of the threats to our people and urge us to be vigilant and protective of our own needs, so too do our people need to hear our stories: the lessons of those of us who have been blessed with a safer life and who have worked to advance the ideals and possibilities life can hold for us and all people. We need to tell **our** stories and to continue to embrace the perspective with which we have been raised.*

I am indebted beyond words to my grandparents for giving me the opportunity to be who I have come to be. I didn't do anything to deserve that gift, but I will not apologize for it. My life in America has been one of Sunday Morning Sunshine and my trip taught me not to take the sun for granted.

I am my grandfather's grandson, and while I will never forget and never abandon my great-uncle and his family's memory, I will always be guided by the sunshine that has graced my life because my grandfather came here. I hope and pray that those of us who have been as fortunate as I have will be grateful for the sunshine that shines on us and find ultimate meaning, self-definition, and obligation in that blessed light.

Of all the sermons I have given, the two included in this chapter are, I feel, among the most important because they reflect the need we all have to wrestle with ourselves and, hopefully, come out of that wrestling match more secure in who we are.

Most importantly, I want my kids, who have recently left the teenage years, to know that the "wrestling" part of life never completely goes away. If we have the right attitude, it will help make our lives as blessed and as meaningful as they could possibly be. We need to grow up but never become so old that we stop questioning who we are.

9

The Bond of Life

Each time I write a sermon, two thoughts come to mind. First, I recall a piece of advice that one of my teachers at rabbinical school gave me: "If the people in the *shul* don't have to hear what you're about to say, don't give the sermon." The sermon has to be important in the minds of the people who hear it.

The second thought I consider is whether I am being true to myself, true to where I have come from, and true to where I am in life. These sermons are, of course, to benefit the congregation, but when I write a sermon, I realize I am writing about myself but for myself as well, and I hope this truth has come through in the previous pages.

So, in conclusion, I offer now what was, in many ways, the most personal sermon I have ever given. It came from the depths of my heart, and although it clearly reached many people, it found a place in my soul as well.

Ironically enough, I wrote this sermon more quickly than I had written any other High Holy Day sermon. I sat down at my laptop while Mickie was at a diving lesson. Before the lesson was over, the sermon was finished and needed no rewrite. When we write from the heart, there is often no need for revisions.

I'll let this sermon be the closing of the book. It is, like this entire volume, about memory and about knowing where we come from and letting that help us to get to where we're going.

REMEMBERING...ALWAYS REMEMBERING
YOM KIPPUR 2008

The number seven is a very meaningful number in Jewish tradition. It connotes completeness. At least it usually does.

It certainly doesn't mean completeness when it is used in connection with sitting shiva. Shiva means seven in Hebrew but when the seven days of mourning have been completed, the mourning process is far from over.

Seven years ago, I stood on this bima on this most sacred day of the year and told you that during the year before I had joined a hevra, a society, a club. It wasn't a club I sought admission to but one which no doubt I anticipated joining at some point in my life.

I had joined a hevra kedoshah, the holy society of mourners.

My father, Manny Dobrusin alav hashalom, had died in March just short of his 80th birthday after a long and worsening series of illnesses. That Yom Kippur morning, I reflected on what the experience of my father's death had meant to me and what I was beginning to learn about being a mourner.

I say "beginning to learn" because, as I said that day, I learned one thing very early in the process of being a mourner: I was never going to lose my membership in that club. Even though shiva would end and even though I would return to more or less the life I always led, I would never stop mourning. Once you are a mourner, you remain a mourner all of your life. I have learned how true that is over the past seven years.

To those of you who have joined this hevra, my sincere condolences to you. I know that it must be difficult to hear me say that you will be a mourner for the rest of your life. But please understand that this is not intended to make your situation more difficult but rather to give you a more positive sense of what it means to be a mourner. This sense will not come immediately but will, someday, bring a new understanding to what it means to mourn.

Now, it is time for a true story.

My story today is about a 53-year-old love affair and the memories it carries. Like the house that is the setting for this story, the story has many different angles and you can choose the one that resonates with you. But please take note that, like so many other significant American stories, it starts and ends with baseball.

I am a loyal, passionate Red Sox fan. I will tell anyone who will listen and even those that won't. My wife and kids know the whole routine by heart. My friends and congregants hear about it more often than they'd like. They've all learned to put up with it.

I was taught to be a Red Sox fan before I knew how to speak. I saw my first game at Fenway Park when I was hardly big enough to walk up the stairs or to see around the pole that was inevitably in front of my seat. The Sox accompanied us always. Our house was filled with the sound of Red Sox baseball on TV or, more likely when I was young, on the radio. If you're a New Englander, you understand.

We lived in the Brighton neighborhood of Boston a few short miles from Fenway. My grandmother bought the house in the late 1940's and my parents moved in with her just after my older brother was born in 1952. I lived in that one house, our house, from the day I was brought home from the hospital until the day I left for college.

On March 6, 2001, my father fell getting out of bed. The paramedics took him to the hospital just to check him out. As it turned out, he required emergency surgery and died in the hospital a week later, never returning home again. He never got to say good-bye to the house.

He also didn't live to see the Sox win a world series. That day he had always dreamed of came three years later, and in late autumn, 2004, I flew back to Boston from Michigan to join the tens of thousands of Red Sox fans who went to the cemetery to leave a Red Sox hat on the grave of someone they love.

In 2002, my mother sold the house to someone who planned to turn it into student apartments. She took one long look at the home she had raised her children in and taken care of her mother and later my father in, and moved out to Michigan to be with us. She never saw the house again.

Every year or so, my brother and I go back to visit our parents' graves and to take a look at the house. One time, we knocked on the door and were invited in. There were a few beer bottles lying around and evidence of a party the night before, but the house seemed like a happy place.

Still, I felt a certain sadness each time I looked at the house. Sure, I missed my parents and I missed my youth, but I also felt sadness for the house itself. I felt like we had abandoned it. I always made it a point to look up to my parents' bedroom window and think of them and it was always hard to turn away and leave. But I had my memories and the house understood, I was sure, that this was the way of the world.

Then Google's "street view" came along. I was a bit concerned. I had read about situations in which there was something embarrassing or inappropriate going on in the picture they posted. I hoped that the house would still look good. After all, this one picture was the reputation that it would carry forever and everywhere.

I couldn't wait. I went to the website, entered our address and a picture came up. The house looked nice, fairly well taken care of, and still the same color. I enlarged the picture and saw into one of the windows just enough to feel like I was inside again and then I zoomed in to look at my parents' bedroom window. I noticed something hanging there.

I took a closer look and could only stare in disbelief. For, thanks to the Internet, the picture that now formed the memory for all who couldn't go to visit it and all who wanted to remember was of our beautiful house with a giant New York Yankees flag hanging out the window.

I am sorry, my dear house. Look what they've done to you. I am sorry that we left you alone. I am so sorry that this is how you will be remembered.

The next summer, I went up to Boston to make my annual visit to the cemeteries where my parents, grandparents, and two great grandparents are buried. I know why I go – to feel the presence of those always in my heart – but I need to stand at the spot of their burial to fulfill my promise to my parents that I would come, and I need, of course, to make sure their headstones are in good shape and their graves taken care of.

But thanks to Ellen's suggestion, I decided to spend a couple of extra days wandering around Massachusetts, driving the backroads I used to travel when I worked at Camp Ramah. So I took days off to drive around exploring. I had a good time and saw some great places, but I was overcome by the feeling that except for the Red Sox, one particular view of the Berkshires, and a piece of Boston pizza, nothing seemed quite the same. I felt a bit like a stranger, especially when I visited Camp Ramah, a place I spent parts of 14 summers. Everything was beautiful but it all looked different from what it was when I was there, and no one remembered me or seemed to care. I can't blame them. It had been many years since I worked there. What I learned was that you can go home again but it won't be the same.

When I was kid, years before "TiVo", I used to think that when I turned off the TV, I could go back to it, turn it on, and pick up the cartoon right where I left it. I learned very quickly that was not the case. But we all think that at times. We think that when we step back from a situation, we can re-inject ourselves right back into it and it won't have changed. Usually, we find we are mistaken.

On a pragmatic level, if we walk away from a situation and leave it in the hands of others, it will look different when we return. When we stop working at a camp for 15 years, of course no one is going to recognize us. When we sell a house, the new owner can do what she wants to do, including putting up a Yankees flag (which by the way, I'm happy to report was not there the next time I returned).

Nothing stays the way we want it to stay in this world. When we walk away, it changes with time. This is what bothered me so much about the house. I didn't want it to be remembered this way. I blamed Google but this is the way of the world.

We have no control over anything that we have left or lost except for two things.

We have a reasonable right to expect that a headstone will not be changed and, more importantly, we have total control over how **we** remember our loved ones.

This is what it means to mourn. We can fix in our minds the memory we want to hold onto, picturing our loved ones as we want to remember them. I'm holding here on the bima the picture of my father the way I want to remember him, a picture taken at a Sunday morning "tallis and tefillin" club minyan at our shul in his corduroy sports jacket with his yarmulke pointed awkwardly, with a happy, contented smile on his face knowing that the breakfast he had just set out with my mother for 20 teenagers and some parents had been properly devoured. That is the picture of him that I have settled on. I also have here a similar image of my mother with a big smile serving dessert at Thanksgiving. These are the ones that I have chosen, and nothing will change them. This is the way they look in my dreams. These images can't be sold, they can't be renovated, they won't be dimmed by time. They are mine. They are locked into me and I am keeping them, to borrow a phrase, in the "bond of life."

Nothing else in life waits for us. Life moves on and well it should. Thank God it does, but the memories of our loved ones stay with us as we want them to. And this is the blessing of memory.

So, let us realize that, as we mourn, a time will come, maybe it will take less than seven years, maybe more, when we will have settled on our image of our loved ones that we want to set in stone like the headstones we placed for them. That memory will be at least a shining ray of light to illuminate and bring comfort to the sadness that will inevitably occasionally bubble up to the surface.

But that does not mean our mourning has come to an end. For mourning is remembering, and mourning is cherishing memories. As long as we care, as long as we cry, as long as we hold onto the memory, that image will keep coming up to bring us comfort.

It is the one thing in life that no one else can touch. It is our private memory and it is ours forever...forever, that is, as long as we allow ourselves the cherished privilege of remembering, and as long as we accept the holy obligation of being, even at our happiest times, even at our times of great satisfaction and comfort, a mourner.

Throughout our lives, in times of joy and sadness, may we always cherish our memories and make sure we choose what to remember. And let those memories help us, in whatever way they can, to teach and inspire others.

So ends this part of my story with, God willing, many more chapters to come.

These long roads have been a joy to experience and a joy to share.